RE-MAKING LOVE

Barbara Ehrenreich's most recent book is *The Hearts of Men: American Dreams and the Flight from Commitment*. Her articles have appeared in many publications, including *The New York Times*, *Vogue*, the *Atlantic* and the *Wall Street Journal*.

Elizabeth Hess is a freelance writer who has written for the *Washington Post*, the *Village Voice*, *Art in America* and *Ms.*, among other publications.

Gloria Jacobs is an editor at *Ms.* Her articles have appeared in such publications as *Mother Jones*, *Woman's World* and the *Daily News*.

D1330703

Barbara Ehrenreich
Elizabeth Hess
Gloria Jacobs

RE-MAKING LOVE

The Feminization of Sex

Fontana/Collins

First published in the USA by Anchor Press/Doubleday 1986
Published in Great Britain by Fontana Paperbacks 1987

Copyright © Barbara Ehrenreich, Elizabeth Hess, Gloria Jacobs 1986

Printed and bound in Great Britain by
William Collins Sons & Co. Ltd, Glasgow

To our children—Alexa, Gideon, Kate,
Rosa, and Benjy—
and to the memory of Betty Ann Colhoun.

Contents

ACKNOWLEDGMENTS

This book was written during a time of exciting new debate on issues of sexuality; the debate has brought argument *and* fresh energy to a discussion that had grown moribund. All of this new work, even when not cited directly in our book, has challenged us and helped to clarify our thinking. Writers such as Dennis Altman, Kate Ellis, Jeffrey Escoffier, Lynne Segal, Christine Stansell, Ann Snitow, Sharon Thompson, Carol Vance, and Ellen Willis have expanded the parameters of the debate and reasserted the importance of sexual liberation within the broader context of women's liberation.

The original idea for this book developed out of an article we wrote for *Ms.* in 1980, and we would like to thank our many friends there for their encouragement and advice.

The numerous women and men who spoke to us about the intimate details of their lives must feel that their reputations are in our hands. We'd like to thank them for their time and their trust in us. In return we have altered their names and some background information to protect their anonymity.

We would like also to thank all the people who offered varied kinds of help, ranging from hours of discussion and shared reading material to typing assistance, computer hookups or a free room to work in. These include Dick Colhoun, Marilyn Gaizband, Lindy Hess, Deborah Huntington, Karen Judd, Mimi Keck, Ellen Keniston, Nancy Lewis Peck, Virginia Reath, Ruth Russell, Brenda Steinberg, Fannie Steinberg, and Stephanie Urdang. John Russell, Harriet Bernstein, and Susan Butler were our extremely able research assistants. In addition, Barbara Ehrenreich thanks the Institute for Policy Studies in Washington, D.C., and the New York Institute for Humanities for providing good fellowship as well as more concrete forms of support.

To our agent, Charlotte Sheedy, and our editor, Loretta Barrett: Both wondered what they were getting into when they took on three authors to do one book. Both knew when to stand back and let us find our way and when to step in with advice and encouragement. We are deeply grateful to each for their deft touch and supportive friendship.

Finally we want to thank Peter Biskind, Jon Steinberg, and Gary Stevenson, who provided sympathetic companionship throughout the many versions of this book. Yes, they changed the diapers, made the dinners, and read and commented on various drafts. Most important, they never considered such support beyond the call of duty.

RE-MAKING LOVE

Introduction

For most Americans, the "sexual revolution" is what Gay Talese found when he set out on his quest to see what middle-aged, middle-class men had been missing all these years: wife-swapping clubs, massage parlors, Hugh Hefner's harem of bunnies, *Screw*. It was a sexual marketplace that dominated and marginalized women; and if this was all there was to the sexual revolution, then its critics have been right to see it as little more than a male fling and a setback for women. The dark side of the gaudy new industry of pornography and commoditized sex for men has been, as feminists have noted, the exploitation of women as "sex workers" (models, masseuses, etc.) and the deepening objectification of *all* women as potential instruments of male pleasure.

But the sexual revolution that Talese found is only half the story, or less. There has been another, hidden sexual revolution that the male commentators and even the feminist critics have for the most part failed to acknowledge: This is a *women's* sexual revolution, and the changes it has brought about in our lives and expectations go far deeper than anything in the superficial spectacle of sexuality we have come to identify as "the" sexual revolution.

In fact, if either sex has gone through a change in sexual attitudes and behavior that deserves to be called revolutionary, it is women, and not men at all. This fact should be widely known, because it leaps out from all the polls and surveys that count for data in these matters. Put briefly, men changed their sexual behavior very little in the decades from the fifties to the eighties. They "fooled around," got married, and often fooled around some more, much as their fathers and perhaps their grandfathers had before them. Women, however, have gone from a pattern of virginity before marriage and monogamy thereafter to a pattern that much more resembles men's: Between the mid-sixties and the mid-seventies, the number of women reporting premarital sexual experience went from a daring minority to a respectable majority; and the proportion of married women reporting active sex lives "on the side" is, in some estimates, close to half. The symbolic importance of female chastity is rapidly disappearing.

It is not only that women came to have more sex, and with a greater variety of partners, but they were having it on their own terms, and enjoying it as enthusiastically as men are said to. As recently as the 1950s, America's greatest acknowledged sexual problem—or as we would now say, "dysfunction"—was female frigidity. Some experts estimated that over half of American women were completely nonorgasmic, or "frigid," and volumes of speculation were devoted to the sources of this unfortunate condition. But in 1975, a *Redbook* survey found that 81 percent of the 100,000 female respondents were orgasmic "all or most of the time."

When a *Cosmopolitan* survey resulted in similar results five years later, writer Linda Wolfe characterized American women, at least those who respond to magazine surveys, as "the most sexually experienced and experimental group of women in Western history."

The statistics on women's sexual revolution may be surprising and unfamiliar, but other evidence of it has become as much a part of the American cultural landscape as shopping malls and video-rental shops. We no longer, for example, expect books offering advice on sex to be the remote, authoritarian works of male physicians. More likely today they are written by women, and based on the experiences of women. Nor do we expect women's sexuality to be simply passive and decorative in its public manifestations. Even in the staid and married suburbs, women flock to male strip joints, provide a market for the new, "couple-oriented" pornographic videotapes, and organize Tupperware-style "home parties" where the offerings are sexual paraphernalia rather than plastic containers. And in media fiction, we no longer find the images of women divided between teasing virgins and sexless matrons: Whether on the prime-time soaps or in the latest teen film, women are likely to be portrayed as sexually assertive, if not downright predatory.

So it is surprising, even somewhat mysterious, that *women's* sexual revolution has been so little heralded, discussed, or even noted. Despite all the evidence as to which sex really changed, the phrase "the sexual revolution" is still more likely to conjure up the image of Hugh Hefner rather than, say, the work of Shere Hite, or to put us in mind of the Times Square smut shops than the expanding sexual marketplace for

women only. One could think of the predictable feminist explanations for why women's sexual revolution,
and only women's, has been so effectively "hidden from
history." This would not be the first time men have
claimed innovations that were originally wrought by
women. Nor would it be the first time men have evaded
a feminine innovation they found vaguely troubling—
or perhaps even overtly disturbing.

But feminists, for the most part, have not been eager
to claim women's sexual revolution either. When they
have acknowledged the change at all, they have tended
to be ambivalent about its meaning for women: To have
more sex, even better sex with men may be liberating
or it may represent no great gain—especially if the men
themselves have evolved so little from the era when
their word for sex was "scoring." But on the whole,
feminists, much like everyone else, have been content
to let "the" sexual revolution mean men's sexual
revolution—and to concentrate on women's roles as
bystanders or victims, not as instigators.

This book is about women's sexual revolution—its
origins in a culture that was repressive not only to sexuality in all its forms but to women as citizens; its connec-
tions, often frayed and tattered, to women's better
known, feminist revolution; its evolution from the optimistic sixties to the much more guarded and conservative eighties. Our focus is on the cultural mainstream—
not the avant-garde and not the brave members of sexual minority groups, most prominently gays and lesbians, who did so much to broaden the American concept
of sexuality. Rather, we are concerned here with the
changes as they occurred in the most obvious places,
the most visible parts of American mass culture, where

strangely, for all their "obviousness," they have been most thoroughly ignored.

Our emphasis, too, is on the cultural implications of women's sexual revolution rather than the raw, demographic indicators of deeper change. It will take another Kinsey to sort through, systematize, and verify the disparate sex surveys of the last two decades. We are less concerned with "how much" than with "what" happened, and—perhaps even more important—how Americans understood and interpreted the change to themselves. Thus, one of our major focuses is on how sex itself changed in the process of women's sexual revolution. It is not that women simply had more sex than they had had in the past, but they began to transform the notion of heterosexual sex itself: from the irreducible "act" of intercourse to a more open-ended and varied kind of encounter. At the same time, the social meaning of sex changed too: from a condensed drama of female passivity and surrender to an interaction between potentially equal persons.

One of our deepest motivating concerns is the relationship between sexual liberation and the larger goals of women articulated by the feminist movement of the past two decades. Feminist ideas, including lesbian feminist ideas, were centrally important to the emergence of women's sexual revolution—even as it has been experienced by women who would never call themselves feminists and who have no sympathy for the gay and lesbian movements. Yet the women's sexual revolution has gone its own way and found itself in settings that are indifferent to feminist concerns and, in some cases, actually hostile to them. The result is, to us, an odd and disturbing separation of goals: Women have won a new range of sexual rights—to pleasure, to fantasy and variety—but we have not yet achieved our full *human* rights. This disjuncture between feminism and women's sexual revolution affects both movements, as we shall see, in ways that are strange and even painful to relate.

The roots of women's sexual revolution lie in a set of circumstances that arose with the waning of the fifties: Middle-class women were beginning to experience the malaise so brilliantly documented by Betty Friedan in *The Feminine Mystique,* and much of their private dissatisfaction centered on marital sex, which fell short of being a glowing payoff for a life of submersion in domestic detail. At the same time, new opportunities were opening up for women. As jobs for women proliferated, young single women crowded into the major cities, and began to enlarge the gap between girlhood and marriage, filling it with careers, romances, and—what was distinctly new—casual sexual adventures. Even very young women were finding, in the burgeoning teen-centered consumer culture, a space of their own between childhood and womanhood. It was these new "spaces"—a teen culture dominated by the heavy beat of rock 'n' roll and a singles culture populated by young, urban adults—that incubated women's sexual revolution.

We begin, perhaps surprisingly, with "Beatlemania," that huge outbreak of teenage female libido that so confounded adults at the time. The experts called it "female hysteria," but it contained the germs of a more serious rebellion against the rules that defined a teenage girl's sexuality as something to be bartered for an early engagement ring. Rock 'n' roll offered a new vision of sexuality (female as well as male) that was distinctly undomesticated; and it offered an unprecedented vision of men, not as beaux or breadwinners but as sex objects for *women*.

In Chapter 2, we move on to the full-scale beginnings of women's sexual revolution, as young, single women began to challenge both the practice and the social interpretation of heterosexual sex. Masters and Johnson have received most of the credit for the new understanding of female sexuality that emerged in the 1960s, but they were, in a way, only providing a scientific rationale for a new social reality that women were creating for themselves. In Chapter 3, we follow the subsequent transformation in the way American culture thought of sex: from a two-stage encounter divided into "foreplay" and intercourse to a far more complex and varied set of possibilities. With sex redefined, the sexual relationship began to be reimagined—not as a spontaneous burst of (mostly male) passion but as an arena for negotiation where women were no longer the automatic losers.

Chapter 4 examines the growing sexual marketplace for women, and the way that the consumer culture has served to perpetuate and proselytize for the women's sexual revolution. Novelty is key to the growth of the sexual marketplace, and it actually encourages practices that were once considered to be marginal and perverted, such as sadomasochism. Nothing could be further from the earlier feminist notions of sexual liberation, yet in one form or another S/M has been assimilated into America's mainstream sexual culture, and not only in its "hard-core," male-oriented expressions. Even stranger, perhaps, is the development we trace in

Chapter 5, the penetration of women's sexual revolution into the otherwise closed-minded culture of right-wing Christian fundamentalism. In this culture, an un-acknowledged kind of sadomasochism is the rule for male-female relationships, yet some covertly feminist notions of sex itself are gaining ground.

While we were researching and writing this book, a backlash against "the" sexual revolution was growing in volume and intensity. The voices raised to denounce the sexual revolution or declare it dead never specify, of course, *whose* revolution is in question. But it seems to us that what inflames the new rhetoric of sexual conservatism must be women's behavior, which *has* changed, rather than men's, which has barely changed at all. Two or three years ago, the critics of sexual revolution focused on what they saw as a loss of "ro-mance" and "meaning," as sex became more casual and less attached to the old consequences—marriage and maternity. Today, arguments for "the death of sex" have gained more force, though not always more scien-tific credibility, by focusing on the danger of AIDS and other venereal diseases. In Chapter 6, we trace the backlash and show how it represents a revival, not only of repressive notions about sexuality but of traditional, sexist notions of women's role in society. We will also find that even as the backlash spreads in the media, more women—from blue- and pink-collar workers to executives—are waging the sexual revolution in their own lives.

We ourselves see much to celebrate in women's sex-ual revolution but also much to reassess and rethink. To us, the greatest problem with this sexual revolution is not that it took away the meaning of sex; if anything, sex has been overly burdened with oppressive "meanings," and especially for women. Nor is it even the threat of disease; historically, sex has always carried risks for women, not the least of which is unwanted pregnancy. Rather, the problem is that women's sexual liberation has become unraveled from the larger theme of women's liberation. For women, sexual equality with men has become a concrete possibility, while economic and social parity remains elusive. We believe it is this fact, beyond all others, that has shaped the possibilities and politics of women's sexual liberation.

To follow and understand this sexual revolution, we ask you to set aside, at least temporarily, both feminist and conservative dogmas about what is good and bad or right and wrong when it comes to sex. The suburban woman who gets her thrills from watching male strippers is paying, with her admission price, to invert the usual relationship between men and women, consumer and object. The born-again Christian woman who imagines her sex life as a service to Jesus has gained purchase to yet another realm of erotic possibilities. At a different end of the cultural spectrum, a practitioner of ritualistic sadomasochism confronts social inequality by encapsulating it in a drama of domination and submission. Desire takes strange paths through a landscape of inequality; we need to be able to follow them, at least in spirit, before we judge.

1

Beatlemania

Girls Just Want to Have Fun

. . . witness the birth of eve—she is rising she
was sleeping she is fading in a naked field
sweating the precious blood of nodding
blooms . . . in the eye of the arena she bends
in half in service—the anarchy that exudes
from the pores of her guitar are the cries of the
people wailing in the rushes . . . a riot of ray/
dios . . .

Patti Smith, "Notice," in Babel

The news footage shows police lines straining against
crowds of hundreds of young women. The police look
grim; the girls' faces are twisted with desperation or, in
some cases, shining with what seems to be an inner
light. The air is dusty from a thousand running and
scuffling feet. There are shouted orders to disperse, answered by a rising volume of chants and wild shrieks.
The young women surge forth; the police line
breaks . . .

Looking at the photos or watching the news clips
today, anyone would guess that this was the sixties—a

demonstration—or maybe the early seventies—the beginning of the women's liberation movement. Until you look closer and see that the girls are not wearing sixties-issue jeans and T-shirts but bermuda shorts, high-necked, preppie blouses, and disheveled but unmistakably bouffant hairdos. This is not 1968 but 1964, and the girls are chanting, as they surge against the police line, "I love Ringo."

Yet, if it was not the "movement," or a clear-cut protest of any kind, Beatlemania was the first mass outburst of the sixties to feature women—in this case girls, who would not reach full adulthood until the seventies and the emergence of a genuinely political movement for women's liberation. The screaming ten- to fourteen-year-old fans of 1964 did not riot *for* anything, except the chance to remain in the proximity of their idols and hence to remain screaming. But they did have plenty to riot against, or at least to overcome through the act of rioting: In a highly sexualized society (one sociologist found that the number of explicitly sexual references in the mass media had doubled between 1950 and 1960), teen and preteen girls were expected to be not only "good" and "pure" but to be the enforcers of purity within their teen society—drawing the line for overeager boys and ostracizing girls who failed in this responsibility. To abandon control—to scream, faint, dash about in mobs—was, in form if not in conscious intent, to protest the sexual repressiveness, the rigid double standard of female teen culture. It was the first and most dramatic uprising of *women's* sexual revolution.

Beatlemania, in most accounts, stands isolated in history as a mere craze—quirky and hard to explain. There had been hysteria over male stars before, but

nothing on this scale. In its peak years—1964 and 1965
—Beatlemania struck with the force, if not the conviction, of a social movement. It began in England with a
report that fans had mobbed the popular but not yet
immortal group after a concert at the London Palla-
dium on October 13, 1963. Whether there was in fact a
mob or merely a scuffle involving no more than eight
girls is not clear, but the report acted as a call to may-
hem. Eleven days later a huge and excited crowd of
girls greeted the Beatles (returning from a Swedish
tour) at Heathrow Airport. In early November, 400
Carlisle girls fought the police for four hours while trying to get tickets for a Beatles concert; nine people
were hospitalized after the crowd surged forward and
broke through shop windows. In London and Birming-
ham the police could not guarantee the Beatles safe
escort through the hordes of fans. In Dublin the police
chief judged that the Beatles' first visit: was "all right
until the mania degenerated into barbarism."[1] And on
the eve of the group's first U.S. tour, *Life* reported, "A
Beatle who ventures out unguarded into the streets
runs the very real peril of being dismembered or
crushed to death by his fans."[2]

When the Beatles arrived in the United States, which
was still ostensibly sobered by the assassination of President Kennedy two months before, the fans knew what
to do. Television had spread the word from England:
The approach of the Beatles is a license to riot. At least
4,000 girls (some estimates run as high as 10,000)
greeted them at Kennedy Airport, and hundreds more
laid siege to the Plaza Hotel, keeping the stars virtual
prisoners. A record 73 million Americans watched the
Beatles on "The Ed Sullivan Show" on February 9,

1964, the night "when there wasn't a hubcap stolen anywhere in America." American Beatlemania soon reached the proportions of religious idolatry. During the Beatles' twenty-three-city tour that August, local promoters were required to provide a minimum of 100 security guards to hold back the crowds. Some cities tried to ban Beatle-bearing craft from their runways; otherwise it took heavy deployments of local police to protect the Beatles from their fans and the fans from the crush. In one city, someone got hold of the hotel pillowcases that had purportedly been used by the Beatles, cut them into 160,000 tiny squares, mounted them on certificates, and sold them for $1 apiece. The group packed Carnegie Hall, Washington's Coliseum and, a year later, New York's 55,600-seat Shea Stadium, and in no setting, at any time, was their music audible above the frenzied screams of the audience. In 1966, just under three years after the start of Beatlemania, the Beatles gave their last concert—the first musical celebrities to be driven from the stage by their own fans.

In its intensity, as well as its scale, Beatlemania surpassed all previous outbreaks of star-centered hysteria. Young women had swooned over Frank Sinatra in the forties and screamed for Elvis Presley in the immediate pre-Beatle years, but the Fab Four inspired an extremity of feeling usually reserved for football games or natural disasters. These baby boomers far outnumbered the generation that, thanks to the censors, had only been able to see Presley's upper torso on "The Ed Sullivan Show." Seeing (whole) Beatles on Sullivan was exciting, but not enough. Watching the band on television was a thrill—particularly the close-ups—but the real goal was to leave home and meet the Beatles. The appropriate reaction to contact with them—such as occupying the same auditorium or city block—was to sob uncontrollably while screaming, "I'm gonna die, I'm gonna die," or, more optimistically, the name of a favorite Beatle, until the onset of either unconsciousness or laryngitis. Girls peed in their pants, fainted, or simply collapsed from the emotional strain. When not in the vicinity of the Beatles—and only a small proportion of fans ever got within shrieking distance of their idols—girls exchanged Beatle magazines or cards, and gathered to speculate obsessively on the details and nuances of Beatle life. One woman, who now administers a Washington, D.C.–based public interest group, recalls long discussions with other thirteen-year-olds in Orlando, Maine:

> I especially liked talking about the Beatles with other girls. Someone would say, "What do you think Paul had for breakfast?" "Do you think he sleeps with a different girl every night?" Or, "Is John really the leader?" "Is George really more sensitive?" And like that for hours.

This fan reached the zenith of junior high school popularity after becoming the only girl in town to travel to a Beatles' concert in Boston: "My mother had made a new dress for me to wear [to the concert] and when I got back, the other girls wanted to cut it up and auction off the pieces."

. To adults, Beatlemania was an affliction, an "epidemic," and the Beatles themselves were only the carriers, or even "foreign germs." At risk were all ten- to fourteen-year-old girls, or at least all white girls; blacks were disdainful of the Beatles' initially derivative and unpolished sound. There appeared to be no cure except for age, and the media pundits were fond of reassuring adults that the girls who had screamed for Frank Sinatra had grown up to be responsible, settled housewives. If there was a shortcut to recovery, it certainly wasn't easy. A group of Los Angeles girls organized a detox effort called "Beatlesaniacs, Ltd.," offering "group therapy for those living near active chapters, and withdrawal literature for those going it alone at far-flung outposts." Among the rules for recovery were: "Do not mention the word Beatles (or beetles)," "Do not mention the word England," "Do not speak with an English accent," and "Do not speak English."[3] In other words, Beatlemania was as inevitable as acne and gum-chewing, and adults would just have to weather it out.

But why was it happening? And why in particular to an America that prided itself on its post-McCarthy maturity, its prosperity, and its clear position as the number one world power? True, there were social problems that not even *Reader's Digest* could afford to be smug about—racial segregation, for example, and the newly discovered poverty of "the other America." But these were things that an energetic President could easily handle—or so most people believed at the time—and if "the Negro problem," as it was called, generated overt unrest, it was seen as having a corrective function and limited duration. Notwithstanding an attempted revival by presidential candidate Barry Goldwater, "extremism" was out of style in any area of expression. In colleges, "coolness" implied a detached and rational appreciation of the status quo, and it was de rigueur among all but the avant-garde who joined the Freedom

Rides or signed up for the Peace Corps. No one, not even Marxist philosopher Herbert Marcuse, could imagine a reason for widespread discontent among the middle class or for strivings that could not be satisfied with a department store charge account—much less for "mania."

In the media, adult experts fairly stumbled over each other to offer the most reassuring explanations. The New York *Times Magazine* offered a "psychological, anthropological," half tongue-in-cheek account, titled "Why the Girls Scream, Weep, Flip." Drawing on the work of the German sociologist Theodor Adorno, *Times* writer David Dempsey argued that the girls weren't really out of line at all; they were merely "conforming." Adorno had diagnosed the 1940s jitterbug fans as "rhythmic obedients," who were "expressing their desire to obey." They needed to subsume themselves into the mass, "to become transformed into an insect." Hence, "jitter*bug,*" and as Dempsey triumphantly added: "Beatles, too, are a type of bug . . . and to 'beatle,' as to jitter, is to lose one's identity in an automatized, insectlike activity, in other words, to obey." If Beatlemania was more frenzied than the outbursts of obedience inspired by Sinatra or Fabian, it was simply because the music was "more frantic," and in some animal way, more compelling. It is generally admitted "that jungle rhythms influence the 'beat' of much contemporary dance activity," he wrote, blithely endorsing the stock racist response to rock 'n' roll. Atavistic, "aboriginal" instincts impelled the girls to scream, weep, and flip, whether they liked it or not: "It is probably no coincidence that the Beatles, who provoke the most violent response among teen-agers, resemble in manner the witch doctors who put their spells on hundreds of shuffling and stamping natives."[4]

Not everyone saw the resemblance between Beatlemanic girls and "natives" in a reassuring light however. *Variety* speculated that Beatlemania might be "a phenomenon closely linked to the current wave of racial rioting."[5] It was hard to miss the element of defiance in Beatlemania. If Beatlemania was conformity, it was conformity to an imperative that overruled adult mores and even adult laws. In the mass experience of Beatlemania, as for example at a concert or an airport, a girl who might never have contemplated shoplifting could assault a policeman with her fists, squirm under police barricades, and otherwise invite a disorderly conduct charge. Shy, subdued girls could go berserk. "Perky," ponytailed girls of the type favored by early sixties sitcoms could dissolve in histrionics. In quieter contemplation of their idols, girls could see defiance in the Beatles or project it onto them. *Newsweek* quoted Pat Hagan, "a pretty, 14-year-old Girl Scout, nurse's aide, and daughter of a Chicago lawyer . . . who previously dug 'West Side Story,' Emily Dickinson, Robert Frost, and Elizabeth Barrett Browning: 'They're tough,' she said of the Beatles. 'Tough is like when you don't conform. . . . You're tumultuous when you're young, and each generation has to have its idols.' "[6] America's favorite sociologist, David Riesman, concurred, describing Beatlemania as "a form of protest against the adult world."[7]

There was another element of Beatlemania that was hard to miss but not always easy for adults to acknowledge. As any casual student of Freud would have noted, at least part of the fans' energy was sexual. Freud's initial breakthrough had been the insight that the epidemic female "hysteria" of the late nineteenth century —which took the form of fits, convulsions, tics, and what we would now call neuroses—was the product of sexual repression. In 1964, though, confronted with massed thousands of "hysterics," psychologists approached this diagnosis warily. After all, despite everything Freud had had to say about childhood sexuality, most Americans did not like to believe that twelve-year-old girls had any sexual feelings to repress. And no normal girl—or full-grown woman, for that matter—was supposed to have the libidinal voltage required for three hours of screaming, sobbing, incontinent, acute-phase Beatlemania. In an article in *Science News Letter* titled "Beatles Reaction Puzzles Even Psychologists," one unidentified psychologist offered a carefully phrased, hygienic explanation: Adolescents are "going through a strenuous period of emotional and physical growth," which leads to a "need for expressiveness, especially in girls." Boys have sports as an outlet; girls have only the screaming and swooning afforded by Beatlemania, which could be seen as "a release of sexual energy."[8]

For the girls who participated in Beatlemania, sex was an obvious part of the excitement. One of the most common responses to reporters' queries on the sources of Beatlemania was, "Because they're sexy." And this explanation was in itself a small act of defiance. It was rebellious (especially for the very young fans) to lay claim to sexual feelings. It was even more rebellious to lay claim to the *active,* desiring side of a sexual attraction: The Beatles were the objects; the girls were their pursuers. The Beatles were sexy; the girls were the ones who perceived them as sexy and acknowledged the force of an ungovernable, if somewhat disembodied, lust. To assert an active, powerful sexuality by the tens of thousands and to do so in a way calculated to attract maximum attention was more than rebellious. It was, in its own unformulated, dizzy way, revolutionary.

SEX AND THE TEENAGE GIRL

In the years and months immediately preceding U.S. Beatlemania, the girls who were to initiate a sexual revolution looked, from a critical adult vantage point, like sleepwalkers on a perpetual shopping trip. Betty Friedan noted in her 1963 classic, *The Feminine Mystique*, "a new vacant sleepwalking, playing-a-part quality of youngsters who do what they are supposed to do, what the other kids do, but do not seem to feel alive or real in doing it."[9] But for girls, conformity meant more than surrendering, comatose, to the banal drift of junior high or high school life. To be popular with boys and girls—to be universally attractive and still have an unblemished "reputation"—a girl had to be crafty, cool, and careful. The payoff for all this effort was to end up exactly like Mom—as a housewife.

In October 1963, the month Beatlemania first broke out in England and three months before it arrived in America, *Life* presented a troubling picture of teenage girl culture. The focus was Jill Dinwiddie, seventeen, popular, "healthy, athletic, getting A grades," to all appearances wealthy, and at the same time, strangely vacant. The pictures of this teenage paragon and her friends would have done justice to John Lennon's first take on American youth:

> When we got here you were all walkin' around in fuckin' Bermuda shorts with Boston crew-cuts and stuff on your teeth. . . . The chicks looked like 1940's horses. There was no conception of dress or any of that jazz. We just thought what an ugly race, what an ugly race.[10]

Jill herself, the "queen bee of the high school," is strikingly sexless: short hair in a tightly controlled style (the kind achieved with flat metal clips), button-down shirts done up to the neck, shapeless skirts with matching cardigans, and a stance that evokes the intense posture-consciousness of prefeminist girls' phys ed. Her philosophy is no less engaging: "We have to be like everybody else to be accepted. Aren't most adults that way? We learn in high school to stay in the middle."[11]

"The middle," for girls coming of age in the early sixties, was a narrow and carefully defined terrain. The omnipresent David Riesman, whom *Life* called in to comment on Jill and her crowd, observed, "Given a standard definition of what is feminine and successful, they must conform to it. The range is narrow, the models they may follow few." The goal, which Riesman didn't need to spell out, was marriage and motherhood, and the route to it led along a straight and narrow path between the twin dangers of being "cheap" or being too puritanical, and hence unpopular. A girl had to learn to offer enough, sexually, to get dates, and at the same time to withhold enough to maintain a boy's interest through the long preliminaries from dating and going steady to engagement and finally marriage. None of this was easy, and for girls like Jill the pedagogical burden of high school was a four-year lesson in how to use sex instrumentally: doling out just enough to be popular with boys and never enough to lose the esteem of the "right kind of kids." Commenting on *Life*'s story on Jill, a University of California sociologist observed:

> It seems that half the time of our adolescent girls is spent trying to meet their new responsibilities to be sexy, glamorous and attractive, while the other half is spent meeting their old responsibility to be virtuous by holding off the advances which testify to their success.

Advice books to teenagers fussed anxiously over the question of "where to draw the line," as did most teenage girls themselves. Officially everyone—girls and advice-givers—agreed that the line fell short of intercourse, though by the sixties even this venerable prohibition required some sort of justification, and the advice-givers strained to impress upon their young readers the calamitous results of premarital sex. First there was the obvious danger of pregnancy, an apparently inescapable danger since no book addressed to teens dared offer birth control information. Even worse, some writers suggested, were the psychological effects of intercourse: It would destroy a budding relationship and possibly poison any future marriage. According to a contemporary textbook titled, *Adolescent Development and Adjustment,* intercourse often caused a man to lose interest ("He may come to believe she is totally promiscuous"), while it was likely to reduce a woman to slavish dependence ("Sometimes a woman focuses her life around the man with whom she first has intercourse").[12] The girl who survived premarital intercourse and went on to marry someone else would find marriage clouded with awkwardness and distrust. Dr. Arthur Cain warned in *Young People and Sex* that the husband of a sexually experienced woman might be consumed with worry about whether his performance matched that of her previous partners. "To make matters worse," he wrote, "it may be that one's sex partner is not as exciting and satisfying as one's previous illicit lover."[13] In short, the price of premarital experience was likely to be postnuptial disappointment. And, since marriage was a girl's peak achievement, an anticlimactic wedding night would be a lasting source of grief.

Intercourse was obviously out of the question, so young girls faced the still familiar problem of where to draw the line on a scale of lesser sexual acts, including (in descending order of niceness): kissing, necking, and petting, this last being divided into "light" (through clothes and/or above the waist) and "heavy" (with clothes undone and/or below the waist). Here the experts were no longer unanimous. Pat Boone, already a spokesman for the Christian right, drew the line at kissing in his popular 1958 book, *'Twixt Twelve and Twenty*. No prude, he announced that "kissing is here to stay and I'm glad of it!" But, he warned, "Kissing is not a game. Believe me! . . . Kissing for fun is like playing with a beautiful candle in a roomful of dynamite!"[14] (The explosive consequences might have been guessed from the centerpiece photos showing Pat dining out with his teen bride, Shirley; then, as if moments later, in a maternity ward with her; and, in the next picture, surrounded by "the four little Boones.") Another pop-singer-turned-adviser, Connie Francis, saw nothing wrong with kissing (unless it begins to "dominate your life"), nor with its extended form, necking, but drew the line at petting:

> Necking and petting—let's get this straight—are two different things. Petting, according to most definitions, is specifically intended to arouse sexual desires and as far as I'm concerned, petting is out for teenagers.[15]

In practice, most teenagers expected to escalate through the scale of sexual possibilities as a relationship progressed, with the big question being: How much, how soon? In their 1963 critique of American teen culture, *Teen-Age Tyranny*, Grace and Fred Hechinger bewailed the cold instrumentality that shaped the conventional answers. A girl's "favors," they wrote, had become "currency to bargain for desirable dates which, in turn, are legal tender in the exchange of popularity." For example, in answer to the frequently asked question, "Should I let him kiss me good night on the first date?" they reported that:

> A standard caution in teen-age advice literature is that, if the boy "gets" his kiss on the first date, he may assume that many other boys have been just as easily compensated. In other words, the rule book advises mainly that the [girl's] popularity assets should be protected against deflation.[16]

It went without saying that it was the girl's responsibility to apply the brakes as a relationship approached the slippery slope leading from kissing toward inter-course. This was not because girls were expected to be immune from temptation. Connie Francis acknowl-edged that "It's not easy to be moral, especially where your feelings for a boy are involved. It never is, because you have to fight to keep your normal physical impulses in line." But it was the girl who had the most to lose, not least of all the respect of the boy she might too gener-ously have indulged. "When she gives in completely to a boy's advances," Francis warned, "the element of re-spect goes right out the window." Good girls never "gave in," never abandoned themselves to impulse or emotion, and never, of course, initiated a new escala-tion on the scale of physical intimacy. In the financial metaphor that dominated teen sex etiquette, good girls "saved themselves" for marriage; bad girls were "cheap."

According to a 1962 Gallup Poll commissioned by *Ladies' Home Journal*, most young women (at least in the *Journal*'s relatively affluent sample) enthusiastically accepted the traditional feminine role and the sexual double standard that went with it:

> Almost all our young women between 16 and 21 expect to be married by 22. Most want 4 children, many want . . . to work until chil-dren come; afterward, a resounding no! They feel a special responsibility for sex *because* they are women. An 18-year-old student in California said, "The standard for men—sow-ing wild oats—results in sown oats. And where does this leave the woman?" . . . Another

student: "A man will go as far as a woman will let him. The girl has to set the standard."[17]

Implicit in this was a matrimonial strategy based on months of sexual teasing (setting the standard), until the frustrated young man broke down and proposed. Girls had to "hold out" because, as one *Journal* respondent put it, "Virginity is one of the greatest things a woman can give to her husband." As for what *he* would give to her, in addition to four or five children, the young women were vividly descriptive:

> . . . I want a split-level brick with four bedrooms with French Provincial cherrywood furniture.
> . . . I'd like a built-in oven and range, counters only 34 inches high with Formica on them.
> . . . I would like a lot of finished wood for warmth and beauty.
> . . . My living room would be long with a high ceiling of exposed beams. I would have a large fireplace on one wall, with a lot of copper and brass around. . . . My kitchen would be very like old Virginian ones—fireplace and oven.

So single-mindedly did young women appear to be bent on domesticity that when Beatlemania did arrive, some experts thought the screaming girls must be auditioning for the maternity ward: "The girls are subconsciously preparing for motherhood. Their frenzied screams are a rehearsal for that moment. Even the jelly babies [the candies favored by the early Beatles and hurled at them by fans] are symbolic."[18] Women were asexual, or at least capable of mentally bypassing sex and heading straight from courtship to reveries of Formica counters and cherrywood furniture, from the soda shop to the hardware store.

But the vision of a suburban split-level, which had guided a generation of girls chastely through high school, was beginning to lose its luster. Betty Friedan had surveyed the "successful" women of her age—educated, upper-middle-class housewives—and found them reduced to infantile neuroticism by the isolation and futility of their lives. If feminism was still a few years off, at least the "feminine mystique" had entered the vocabulary, and even Jill Dinwiddie must have read the quotation from journalist Shana Alexander that appeared in the same issue of *Life* that featured Jill. "It's a marvelous life, this life in a man's world," Alexander said. "I'd climb the walls if I had to live the feminine mystique." The media that had once romanticized togetherness turned their attention to "the crack in the picture window"—wife swapping, alcoholism, divorce, and teenage anomie. A certain cynicism was creeping into the American view of marriage. In the novels of John Updike and Philip Roth, the hero didn't get the girl, he got away. When a Long Island prostitution ring, in which housewives hustled with their husbands' consent, was exposed in the winter of 1963, a Fifth Avenue saleswoman commented: "I see all this beautiful stuff I'll never have, and I wonder if it's worth it to be good. What's the difference, one man every night or a different man?"[19]

So when sociologist Bennet Berger commented in *Life* that "there is nobody better equipped than Jill to live in a society of all-electric kitchens, wall-to-wall carpeting, dishwashers, garbage disposals [and] color TV," this could no longer be taken as unalloyed praise. Jill herself seemed to sense that all the tension and teasing anticipation of the teen years was not worth the payoff. After she was elected, by an overwhelming majority, to the cheerleading team, "an uneasy, faraway look clouded her face." "I guess there's nothing left to do in high school," she said. "I've made song leader both years, and that was all I really wanted." For girls, high school was all there was to public life, the only place you could ever hope to run for office or experience the quasi fame of popularity. After that came marriage—most likely to one of the crew-cut boys you'd made out with —then isolation and invisibility.

Part of the appeal of the male star—whether it was James Dean or Elvis Presley or Paul McCartney—was that you would *never* marry him; the romance would never end in the tedium of marriage. Many girls expressed their adulation in conventional, monogamous terms, for example, picking their favorite Beatle and writing him a serious letter of proposal, or carrying placards saying, "John, Divorce Cynthia." But it was inconceivable that any fan would actually marry a Beatle or sleep with him (sexually active "groupies" were still a few years off) or even hold his hand. Adulation of the male star was a way to express sexual yearnings that would normally be pressed into the service of popularity or simply repressed. The star could be loved noninstrumentally, for his own sake, and with complete abandon. To publicly advertise this hopeless love was to protest the calculated, pragmatic sexual repression of teenage life.

THE ECONOMICS OF MASS HYSTERIA

Sexual repression had been a feature of middle-class teen life for centuries. If there was a significant factor that made mass protest possible in the late fifties (Elvis) and the early sixties (the Beatles), it was the growth and maturation of a teen market: for distinctly teen clothes, magazines, entertainment, and accessories. Consciousness of the teen years as a life-cycle phase set off between late childhood on the one hand and young adulthood on the other only goes back to the early twentieth century, when the influential psychologist G. Stanley Hall published his mammoth work *Adolescence*. (The word "teenager" did not enter mass usage until the 1940s.) Postwar affluence sharpened the demarcations around the teen years: Fewer teens than ever worked or left school to help support their families, making teenhood more distinct from adulthood as a time of unemployment and leisure. And more teens than ever had money to spend, so that from a marketing viewpoint, teens were potentially much more interesting than children, who could only influence family spending but did little spending themselves. Grace and Fred Hechinger reported that in 1959 the average teen spent $555 on "goods and services not including the necessities normally supplied by their parents," and noted, for perspective, that in the same year schoolteachers in Mississippi were earning just over $3,000. "No matter what other segments of American society— parents, teachers, sociologists, psychologists, or policemen—may deplore the power of teenagers," they observed, "the American business community has no cause for complaint."[20]

If advertisers and marketing men manipulated teens as consumers, they also, inadvertently, solidified teen culture against the adult world. Marketing strategies that recognized the importance of teens as precocious consumers also recognized the importance of heightening their self-awareness of themselves *as teens*. Girls especially became aware of themselves as occupying a world of fashion of their own—not just bigger children's clothes or slimmer women's clothes. You were not a big girl or a junior woman, but a "teen," and in that notion lay the germs of an oppositional identity. Defined by its own products and advertising slogans, teenhood became more than a prelude to adulthood; it was a status to be proud of—emotionally and sexually complete unto itself.

Rock 'n' roll was the most potent commodity to enter the teen consumer subculture. Rock was originally a black musical form with no particular age identification, and it took white performers like Buddy Holly and Elvis Presley to make rock 'n' roll accessible to young white kids with generous allowances to spend. On the white side of the deeply segregated music market, rock became a distinctly teenage product. Its "jungle beat" was disconcerting or hateful to white adults; its lyrics celebrated the special teen world of fashion ("Blue Suede Shoes"), feeling ("Teenager in Love"), and passive opposition ("Don't know nothin' 'bout his-to-ry"). By the late fifties, rock 'n' roll was the organizing principle and premier theme of teen consumer culture: You watched the Dick Clark show not only to hear the hits but to see what the kids were wearing; you collected not only the top singles but the novelty items that advertised the stars; you cultivated the looks and person-

ality that would make you a "teen angel." And if you
were still too young for all this, in the late fifties you
yearned to grow up to be—not a woman and a housewife, but a teenager.

Rock 'n' roll made mass hysteria almost inevitable: It
announced and ratified teen sexuality and then ampli-
fied teen sexual frustration almost beyond endurance.
Conversely, mass hysteria helped make rock 'n' roll. In
his biography of Elvis Presley, Albert Goldman de-
scribes how Elvis's manager, Colonel Tom Parker,
whipped mid-fifties girl audiences into a frenzy before
the appearance of the star: As many as a dozen acts
would precede Elvis—acrobats, comics, gospel singers,
a little girl playing a xylophone—until the audience,
"driven half mad by sheer frustration, began chanting
rhythmically, '*We want Elvis, we want Elvis!*' " When
the star was at last announced:

> Five thousand shrill female voices come in on
> cue. The screeching reaches the intensity of a
> jet engine. When Elvis comes striding out on-
> stage with his butchy walk, the screams sud-
> denly escalate. They switch to hyperspace.
> Now, you may as well be stone deaf for all the
> music you'll hear.[21]

The newspapers would duly report that "the fans went
wild."

Hysteria was critical to the marketing of the Beatles.
First there were the reports of near riots in England.
Then came a calculated publicity tease that made Colo-
nel Parker's manipulations look oafish by contrast: Five
million posters and stickers announcing "The Beatles
Are Coming" were distributed nationwide. Disc jock-

eys were blitzed with promo material and Beatle interview tapes (with blank spaces for the DJ to fill in the
questions, as if it were a real interview) and enlisted in a
mass "countdown" to the day of the Beatles' arrival in
the United States. As Beatle chronicler Nicholas Schaffner reports:

> Come break of "Beatle Day," the quartet had
> taken over even the disc-jockey patter that
> punctuated their hit songs. From WMCA and
> WINS through W-A-Beatle-C, it was "thirty
> Beatle degrees," "eight-thirty Beatle time"
> . . . [and] "four hours and fifty minutes to
> go."[22]

By the time the Beatles materialized, on "The Ed Sullivan Show" in February 1964, the anticipation was un-
bearable. A woman who was a fourteen-year-old in Du-
luth at the time told us, "Looking back, it seems so
commercial to me, and so degrading that millions of us
would just scream on cue for these four guys the media
dangled out in front of us. But at the time it was something intensely personal for me and, I guess, a million
other girls. The Beatles seemed to be speaking directly
to us and, in a funny way, *for us.*"

By the time the Beatles hit America, teens and
preteens had already learned to look to their unique
consumer subculture for meaning and validation. If this
was manipulation—and no culture so strenuously and
shamelessly exploits its children as consumers—it was
also subversion. *Bad* kids became juvenile delinquents,
smoked reefers, or got pregnant. Good kids embraced
the paraphernalia, the lore, and the disciplined fandom
of rock 'n' roll. (Of course, bad kids did their thing to a

rock beat too: the first movie to use a rock 'n' roll sound-track was "Blackboard Jungle," in 1955, cementing the suspected link between "jungle rhythms" and teen re-bellion.) For girls, fandom offered a way not only to sublimate romantic and sexual yearnings but to carve out subversive versions of heterosexuality. Not just any-one could be hyped as a suitable object for hysteria: It *mattered* that Elvis was a grown-up greaser, and that the Beatles let their hair grow over their ears.

THE EROTICS OF THE STAR-FAN RELATIONSHIP

In real life, i.e. in junior high or high school, the ideal boyfriend was someone like Tab Hunter or Ricky Nel-son. He was "all boy," meaning you wouldn't get home from a date without a friendly scuffle, but he was also clean-cut, meaning middle class, patriotic, and respect-ful of the fact that good girls waited until marriage. He wasn't moody and sensitive (like James Dean in *Giant* or *Rebel Without a Cause),* he was realistic (meaning that he understood that his destiny was to earn a living for someone like yourself). The stars who inspired the greatest mass adulation were none of these things, and their very remoteness from the pragmatic ideal was what made them accessible to fantasy.

Elvis was visibly lower class and symbolically black (as the bearer of black music to white youth). He repre-sented an unassimilated white underclass that had been forgotten by mainstream suburban America—or, more accurately, he represented a middle-class caricature of

poor whites. He was *sleazy*. And, as his biographer
Goldman argues, therein lay his charm:

> What did the girls see that drove them out of
> their minds? It sure as hell wasn't the All-
> American Boy. . . . Elvis was the flip side of
> [the] conventional male image. His fish-belly
> white complexion, so different from the
> "healthy tan" of the beach boys; his brooding
> Latin eyes, heavily shaded with mascara . . .
> the thick, twisted lips; the long, greasy hair.
> . . . God! what a freak the boy must have
> looked to those little girls . . . and what a
> turn-on! Typical comments were: "I like him
> because he looks so mean" . . . "He's been in
> and out of jail."[23]

Elvis stood for a dangerous principle of masculinity that
had been expunged from the white-collar, split-level
world of fandom: a hood who had no place in the
calculus of dating, going steady, and getting married.
At the same time, the fact that he was lower class
evened out the gender difference in power. He acted
arrogant, but he was really vulnerable, and would be
back behind the stick shift of a Mack truck if you, the
fans, hadn't redeemed him with your love. His very
sleaziness, then, was a tribute to the collective power of
the teen and preteen girls who worshipped him. He
was obnoxious to adults—a Cincinnati used-car dealer
once offered to smash fifty Presley records in the presence of every purchaser—not only because of who he
was but because he was a reminder of the emerging
power and sexuality of young girls.

Compared to Elvis, the Beatles were almost respectable. They wore suits; they did not thrust their bodies about suggestively; and to most Americans, who couldn't tell a blue-collar, Liverpudlian accent from Oxbridge English, they might have been upper class. What was both shocking and deeply appealing about the Beatles was that they were, while not exactly effeminate, at least not easily classifiable in the rigid gender distinctions of middle-class American life. Twenty years later we are so accustomed to shoulder-length male tresses and rock stars of ambiguous sexuality that the Beatles of 1964 look clean-cut. But when the Beatles arrived at crew-cut, precounterculture America, their long hair attracted more commentary than their music. Boy fans rushed to buy Beatle wigs and cartoons showing well-known male figures decked with Beatle hair were a source of great merriment. *Playboy,* in an interview, grilled the Beatles on the subject of homosexuality, which it was only natural for gender-locked adults to suspect. As Paul McCartney later observed:

> There they were in America, all getting house-trained for adulthood with their indisputable principle of life: short hair equals men; long hair equals women. Well, we got rid of that small convention for them. And a few others, too.[24]

What did it mean that American girls would go for these sexually suspect young men, and in numbers far greater than an unambiguous stud like Elvis could command? Dr. Joyce Brothers thought the Beatles' appeal rested on the girls' innocence:

> The Beatles display a few mannerisms which almost seem a shade on the feminine side, such as the tossing of their long manes of hair. . . . These are exactly the mannerisms which very young female fans (in the 10-to-14 age group) appear to go wildest over.[25]

The reason? "Very young 'women' are still a little frightened of the idea of sex. Therefore they feel safer worshipping idols who don't seem too masculine, or too much the 'he man.' "

What Brothers and most adult commentators couldn't imagine was that the Beatles' androgyny was itself sexy. "The idea of sex" as intercourse, with the possibility of pregnancy or a ruined reputation, was indeed frightening. But the Beatles construed sex more generously and playfully, lifting it out of the rigid scenario of mid-century American gender roles, and it was this that made them wildly sexy. Or to put it the other way around, the appeal lay in the vision of sexuality that the Beatles held out to a generation of American girls: They seemed to offer sexuality that was guileless, ebullient, and fun—like the Beatles themselves and everything they did (or were shown doing in their films *Help* and *A Hard Day's Night).* Theirs was a vision of sexuality freed from the shadow of gender inequality because the group mocked the gender distinctions that bifurcated the American landscape into "his" and "hers." To Americans who believed fervently that sexuality hinged on *la différence,* the Beatlemaniacs said, No, blur the lines and expand the possibilities.

At the same time, the attraction of the Beatles bypassed sex and went straight to the issue of power. Our informant from Orlando, Maine, said of her Beatle-manic phase:

> It didn't feel sexual, as I would now define that.
> It felt more about wanting freedom. I didn't
> want to grow up and be a wife and it seemed to
> me that the Beatles had the kind of freedom I
> wanted: No rules, they could spend two days
> lying in bed; they ran around on motorbikes,
> ate from room service. . . . I didn't want to
> sleep with Paul McCartney, I was too young.
> But I wanted to be like them, something larger
> than life.

Another woman, who was thirteen when the Beatles arrived in her home city of Los Angeles and was working for the telephone company in Denver when we interviewed her, said:

> Now that I've thought about it, I think I identi-
> fied with them, rather than as an object of
> them. I mean I liked their independence and
> sexuality and wanted those things for myself.
> . . . Girls didn't get to be that way when I was
> a teenager—we got to be the limp, passive ob-
> ject of some guy's fleeting sexual interest. We
> were so stifled, and they made us meek, giggly
> creatures think, oh, if only *I* could act that way,
> and be strong, sexy, and doing what you want.

If girls could not be, or ever hope to be, superstars and madcap adventurers themselves, they could at least idolize the men who were.

There was the more immediate satisfaction of know-ing, subconsciously, that the Beatles were who they were because girls like oneself had made them that. As with Elvis, fans knew of the Beatles' lowly origins and knew they had risen from working-class obscurity to world fame on the acoustical power of thousands of shrieking fans. Adulation created stars, and stardom, in turn, justified adulation. Questioned about their hysteria, some girls answered simply, "Because they're the Beatles." That is, because they're who I happen to like. And the louder you screamed, the less likely anyone would forget the power of the fans. When the screams drowned out the music, as they invariably did, then it was the fans, and not the band, who were the show.

In the decade that followed Beatlemania, the girls who had inhabited the magical, obsessive world of fandom would edge closer and closer to center stage. Sublimation would give way to more literal, and sometimes sordid, forms of fixation: By the late sixties, the most zealous fans, no longer content to shriek and sob in virginal frustration, would become groupies and "go all the way" with any accessible rock musician. One briefly notorious group of girl fans, the Chicago Plaster Casters, distinguished itself by making plaster molds of rock stars' penises, thus memorializing, among others, Jimi Hendrix. At the end of the decade Janis Joplin, who had been a lonely, unpopular teenager in the fifties, shot to stardom before dying of a drug and alcohol overdose. Joplin, before her decline and her split from Big Brother, was in a class by herself. There were no other female singers during the sixties who reached her pinnacle of success. Her extraordinary power in the male world of rock 'n' roll lay not only in her talent but in her femaleness. While she did not meet conventional standards of beauty, she was nevertheless sexy and powerful; both genders could worship her on the stage for their own reasons. Janis offered women the possibility of identifying with, rather than objectifying, the star. "It was seeing Janis Joplin," wrote Ellen Willis, "that made me resolve, once and for all, not to get my hair straightened." Her "metamorphosis from the ugly duckling of Port Arthur to the peacock of Haight Ashbury"[26] gave teenage girls a new optimistic fantasy.

While Janis was all woman, she was also one of the boys. Among male rock stars, the faintly androgynous affect of the Beatles was quickly eclipsed by the frank bisexuality of performers like Alice Cooper and David Bowie, and then the more outrageous antimasculinity of eighties stars Boy George and Michael Jackson. The latter provoked screams again and mobs, this time of interracial crowds of girls, going down in age to eight and nine, but never on the convulsive scale of Beatlemania. By the eighties, female singers like Grace Jones and Annie Lenox were denying gender too, and the loyalty and masochism once requisite for female lyrics gave way to new songs of cynicism, aggression, exultation. But between the vicarious pleasure of Beatlemania and Cyndi Lauper's forthright assertion in 1984 that "girls just want to have fun," there would be an enormous change in the sexual possibilities open to women and girls—a change large enough to qualify as a "revolution."

2
Up from the Valley of the Dolls
The Origins of the Sexual Revolution

Anne Welles's personal sexual revolution was indistinguishable from her rebellion, in an unconsciously feminist fashion, against the rigid sex roles of small-town America. Anne was the heroine of Jacqueline Susann's 1966 best-seller, *Valley of the Dolls,* and for Anne, like Susann herself, the big city—in both cases, New York—promised freedom and inexhaustible adventure:

> She would *never* go back to Lawrenceville!
> . . . She had escaped. Escaped from marriage
> to some solid Lawrenceville boy, from the
> solid, orderly life of Lawrenceville. The same
> orderly life her mother had lived. And her
> mother's mother. In the same orderly kind of a
> house. A house that a good New England fam-

ily had lived in generation after generation, its inhabitants smothered with orderly, unused emotions, emotions stifled beneath the creaky iron armor called "manners."[1]

In no small part, it was the sexlessness of life in Lawrenceville that drove Anne to a cramped apartment and an uncertain secretarial career in New York. She recalls asking her mother, "When a man takes you in his arms and kisses you, it should be wonderful, shouldn't it? Wasn't it ever wonderful with Daddy?" To which her mother replies stiffly, "Unfortunately, kissing isn't all a man expects after marriage."

In 1966–67 the media began to talk about "the sexual revolution," and the sexual playfulness of the emerging counterculture was only one element of the change. Novels like *Valley of the Dolls,* which seemed at the time to border on pornography, were themselves a sign of the "revolution." *Human Sexual Response,* by Dr. William Masters and Virginia Johnson, also published in 1966, was to become one of its major ideological manifestos. The women's liberation movement and the mass spread of feminist consciousness were still two or three years ahead, but the designation of a sexual "revolution" implied a change that went beyond manners and mores to fundamental relationships of power. Women's sexual revolution grew out of the same frustrations and emerging opportunities that inspired the feminist movement and, like it, initially represented the aspirations of the "new woman"—urban, single, educated—who had to overcome both the puritanism of small-town America and the smothering conformity of suburban married life.

By the early sixties, thousands of young women, like the fictional Anne Welles, were rejecting the lockstep sequence that led from college or high school graduation directly to marriage and maternity. They expected to spend a few years on their own, working and dating, and not just as a way of passing time until "Mr. Right" arrived. Being single had its own rewards, especially in a city packed with other young people and far from parental oversight. While the teens and preteens were still shrieking over the Beatles—and anticipating a more adventurous sexuality—young women in their twenties were already carving out a new kind of sexual identity. Sex had been defined as an adjunct to marriage, as a means to getting married, and as proof of a "mature acceptance of the female role." But for women who were trying out new roles, even on a temporary basis, the old rules and definitions would not do.

The birth control pill, which first became commercially available in 1960, contributed to women's sexual revolution but by no means *caused* it. The causes of the sexual revolution were more sociological than technological: Without a concentration of young, single women in the cities, there would have been no sexual revolution. But without the pill, there would still have been the diaphragm; and for many young women who came of age in the prepill years, that first diaphragm, discreetly packed in purse or college book bag, was both the symbol and the instrument of sexual liberation. The pill was more convenient—though, as women were to discover later in the decade, it was also far more hazardous than the diaphragm. But its real function was, in a sense, to legitimize a sexual revolution already in progress: The existence and widespread marketing of a technology for presumably effortless contraception was evidence that millions of women (almost 6 million by 1965), single as well as married, were "doing it"—and, apparently with the blessings of the medical profession, getting away with it too.

THE CRISIS OF MARRIED LOVE

The sexual revolution reflected not only the opportunities opening up to the "new," single women, but the discontent of the married majority. The only officially acceptable setting for an active sex life was still the bedroom—in a house, preferably a new suburban split-level, not a makeshift apartment. Outside of a small avant-garde, most young women still expected their single years to culminate in marriage, which, ideally, would be a source not only of financial security but of companionship and sexual fulfillment. But by the early sixties, it was clear that all was not well even within the "ideal" marriages of well-adjusted, educated, middle-class women. To Betty Friedan, who remains our best chronicler of such women's frustrations on the eve of the feminist revival, it seemed that a sexual revolution, of a fairly nasty and unrewarding type, had already taken place by the early sixties. The housewives she surveyed for *The Feminine Mystique* seemed to be pouring the energies that might have gone into careers or other "larger human purposes" into a vacant and obsessive search for sexual fulfillment. "The mounting sex-hunger of American women has been documented ad nauseam," she wrote, and was reflected in the salaciousness of best-sellers addressed to women *(Peyton*

Place was the most egregious example), and what she saw as a "joyless" preoccupation with sexual technique.[2]

The changes Friedan perceived had less to do with actual sexual practice than with the way women thought about sex and the emotional intensity they brought to the subject. She attributed the new way of thinking about sex in large part to the Kinsey reports, both what they reported "and the way they reported it"—which was dryly, and with masses of statistics, as if sex had nothing to do with human feelings. Like most critics of Kinsey (and later, of Masters and Johnson), she believed that a purely scientific approach to human sexuality was necessarily depersonalizing and possibly an invitation to licentiousness. The Kinsey reports (one on male sexuality, in 1948, and one on female sexuality, in 1953) "reduced [sexuality] to its narrowest physiological limits." In particular, Friedan observed, they treated "sexuality as a status-seeking game in which the goal was the greatest number of 'outlets,' [or] orgasms."[3]

In fact, the "discourse" on sexuality—the collective way of thinking and talking about it—had been shifting decisively throughout the post–World War II period. The vague references to sexual "satisfaction" or "fulfillment" that had characterized sexological writing earlier in the century were being replaced by a one-word description of a physiological event—"orgasm." In part, the new emphasis on the orgasm as the touchstone of sexual experience came from the émigré psychoanalyst Wilhelm Reich, who attributed the orgasm with a mystical, redemptive power to heal and inspire. His influence, however, was largely limited to an intellectual avant-garde. Most Americans learned to think of sex in terms of orgasms from Kinsey, and his interest in them was far more prosaic than Reich's. A scientist, Alfred Kinsey was determined to make his study of sex quantitatively precise; and that meant he needed some way to measure the amorphous notion of sexual experience. He needed something to *count*, and what he chose to count was orgasms.

The Kinsey reports were sensational for their revelations about the sheer volume of extramarital and often deviant sex in pre–sexual-revolution America. But it was his methodology, rather than his findings, that had a lasting effect on how Americans think about sex. His focus on the orgasm count—as opposed to, say, the number of "affairs" or "acts of penetration"—carried with it the implicit notion that all routes to orgasm are somehow equivalent or at least equally worthy of note. Sex, as studied by Kinsey and his colleagues, did not necessarily include love, heterosexual attraction, or even any human interaction. It included homosexual sex, masturbation, and even bestiality—all of which were horrifyingly deviant but which nonetheless showed up in the bottom line, the orgasm count. The latent message, which did not achieve widespread acceptance for decades, was that if we were to be objective about sex, we would have to learn to be a little less judgmental about how it was defined.

Another message, which was much more readily absorbed even in the fifties, was that men and women were not so different sexually after all. In *Sexual Behavior in the Human Female,* Kinsey and his colleagues asserted that in spite of the widespread and oft-repeated emphasis on the supposed differences between female and male sexuality, we fail to find any anatomic or physiological basis for such differences.[4]

In particular, "orgasm is a phenomenon which appears to be essentially the same in the human female and male." These conclusions contradicted the dominant, Freudian theories of female sexuality that still prevailed in most popularly available information and advice, but they were hard to ignore. If sexology was a science, and if the orgasm was its principle "unit of measurement," then surely women's orgasms had to "count" as much as men's.

The Kinsey reports encouraged women to take a more hardheaded—the critics said "selfish"—view of sex. Vaguer descriptions of sexual pleasure, like "satisfaction" or "fulfillment," could easily be confused with intangible feelings of love and affection. But orgasm was a definite event; it could happen quite independently of any human feeling. Thus sex was not just an extension of love but a separate realm within which a marriage could either falter or succeed. Within this realm, there was little ambiguity: While a woman might be aware of more or less "satisfaction," she could actually count orgasms. If American women were beginning to think of sex as a "status-seeking game," as Friedan worried, there was now a way to tally the score.

In popular, as well as expert opinion, American women did not measure up very well. Physicians believed that over 50 percent of American women were "frigid"[5] a condition which had expanded to include not only those who were totally unresponsive but those who failed to have orgasms. In medical literature, frigidity emerged in the fifties as a major health problem, the presumptive cause of a range of gynecological disorders from menstrual pain to infertility. To the average female, "frigidity" was a judgment freighted with a variety of resentments: that American women dominated their men (an inexhaustible theme in popular magazines); that American men were being "emasculated" by everything from the corporate work world to the suburban barbecue (a major motif of fifties' sociology); that the average wife was in fact a sexless creature compared to the cone-breasted Hollywood ideal of femininity. No wonder, then, that Friedan's informants seemed so joylessly preoccupied with their sexual status —their self-worth was at stake. In *Valley of the Dolls*, Anne's first tentative sexual encounter leads to agonizing introspection:

> Something was wrong with her. Why should she feel this cold distaste at a man's kiss? . . . She was deep in her own thoughts as they drove home. She knew the awful truth now. She was frigid. That awful word the girls in school used to whisper about. Some girls were born that way—they never reached a climax or felt any real passion. And she was one of them.

Anne's problem, however, was uncomplicated: She had not yet truly fallen in love. With the right man, the dapper and unreliable Lyon, she is finally able to report that "it happened," admitting, "I was beginning to worry about myself." Reassuringly he tells her, "Not at all—it's very rare for a girl to actually feel anything or reach a climax in the beginning." In response, "she kissed his face eagerly. 'I function, Lyon—I'm a woman!' "[6]

In the Freud-tinged sexual theories that most women were likely to encounter in magazine advice columns, orgasm—that is, vaginal orgasm during intercourse— was an important proof of womanhood. But, frustratingly, there seemed to be nothing a woman could actually *do* to achieve one. The available sex manuals—or "marriage manuals" as they were then known— stressed both the necessity of achieving orgasm and its total dependence on male effort. (It did not matter to the advice-givers that Kinsey and his research colleagues had publicized alternative routes to female orgasm, such as masturbation and lesbian sex. In the Freudian view, those were "immature" and deviant forms of female sexuality.) In the most widely read manual of the fifties, *Ideal Marriage: Its Physiology and Technique*, by the Dutch physician Th. H. Van de Velde (the book was originally published in the United States in 1930 and went through thirty-two reprints between 1941 and 1957), orgasm was described as a physiological requirement—at least for any woman who had set out on the path to coitus. According to Van de Velde, failure to relieve the "congestion" created in the first stages of sexual arousal would lead immediately to "nervous anger, fatigue, malaise, and pain" and, over time, to a variety of gynecological disorders, including painful and irregular menstruation and "vague or definite localized or wandering pains." Thus there were sound medical reasons why men had to strive to satisfy their wives, for as he warned repeatedly, and in italics:

> *Every considerable erotic stimulation of their*
> *wives that does not terminate in orgasm, on*
> *the woman's part, represents an injury, and*
> *repeated injuries of this kind lead to perma-*
> *nent—or very obstinate—damage to both*
> *body and soul.*[7]

It was Van de Velde's zealous insistence on female orgasm (not merely "pleasure" but orgasm) that en-
deared him to female readers and no doubt contributed
to what Betty Friedan deplored as the "mounting sex
hunger" of American women.

But in the sex act described by Van de Velde and his
numerous, easy-to-read imitators in the fifties, women
were barely participants, much less full "partners." The
man was to set the pace, introduce innovations, and
decide when foreplay would end and the real business
of penetration would begin; the woman had only to
respond. Van de Velde did not even think women were
a worthwhile audience for his fund of knowledge, and
addressed *Ideal Marriage* to physicians and "married
men," explaining that the latter "are naturally educa-
tors and initiators of their wives in sexual matters."[8]
Nor could women be useful sources of information, for
example on the experience of orgasm, since "only few
women are at present capable of observing and recording their own sensations, and then subsequently of ana-
lyzing them." Officially, then, women were barred
from the discourse on sex. They had nothing to say and
no reason to be told anything, and whatever they felt
was the product of male effort. When women's role in
the sex act had to be explicated, Van de Velde and his
successors drew on Balzac's musical analogy: "Woman

is a harp who only yields her secrets of melody to the master who knows how to handle her."[9]

As to how a man was to achieve this degree of virtuosity, the pre–sexual-revolution manuals were either vague or misleading. At times, for example, Van de Velde acknowledged the importance of clitoral stimulation (without, however, offering much advice on how to accomplish it), and at times he wrote as if the female orgasm would be triggered automatically by the "refreshing" flow of the male ejaculation. Another popular advice book, *A Marriage Manual* by Drs. Hannah and Abraham Stone (but written in the third person singular, "Doctor"), advised manual stimulation of the clitoris only as a last-ditch effort, to be undertaken after "normal sexual union" had failed to produce a female orgasm.* And, having gone this far, the Stones felt constrained to have their imaginary interlocutor (a frequent character in sex manuals) inquire, "Wouldn't such a practice be a perversion, Doctor?"[10]

Van de Velde believed that male dominance in sex was completely "natural," but not so natural that couples did not have to be warned against more egalitarian modes of expression. Thus he found it necessary to caution against having the woman too frequently on top during intercourse, a position he felt encouraged "the

---

* Writing years later, but still untouched by any sexual revolution, Dr. David Reuben undertook to define the male responsibility for female orgasm in scientifically quantitative terms:

> No woman deserves to be labeled sexually frigid unless her sexual partner provides her with at least enough mechanical stimulation to trigger the orgasmic response.
>
> *How much stimulation is that?* For the average couple, about eight minutes of actual intercourse or seventy-five to eighty pelvic thrusts.[11]

complete passivity of the man and the exclusive activity
of his partner." This, he wrote, "is directly contrary to
the natural relationship of the sexes, and must bring
unfavorable consequences if it becomes habitual." In
another place he tells us that "on purely aesthetic
grounds," male passivity in sex "is out of the question
for men of white Western races in modern civiliza-
tion."[12]

In fact, for Van de Velde, it was not enough to estab-
lish the aesthetic superiority of male leadership in sex;
he seemed driven to suppress all signs, however involuntary, of female initiative. Female *movements* during
coitus (the notion was strange enough to italicize) were
contraindicated on the ground that "with too vigorous
[female] motion, the intromittent organ slips out of the
vagina"—a most embarrassing sidetrack. Female initiative in "genital kissing" was discouraged for reasons of
"delicacy" and "discretion." Female sounds were another potential problem, and provided the basis for a
bizarre argument against rear-entry positions, which
might otherwise have been assumed to guarantee male
"mastery":

> The piston-like backwards and forwards mo-
> tion of the phallus may occasionally force some
> of the air out of the vaginal cavity again, to the
> accompaniment of unpleasantly suggestive
> and quite audible whistling sounds. Even
> when the air leaves the vagina again on the
> assumption of a more normal position after
> intercourse . . . the process is only too audi-
> ble and extraordinarily repulsive in its effect.[13]

Here the ancient fear of the "toothed vagina" has been extended to the repulsive possibility of a talking vagina —genitalia which might appear to have a life of their own, independent of a woman's "natural" reticence and submissiveness.

So much did the sex act depend on male agency and female passivity that Van de Velde and his contemporaries rarely referred to the participants as "partners"—a usage which became widespread only in the sixties. In their misogynist classic of 1947, *Modern Woman: The Lost Sex*, which was influential well into the fifties, Ferdinand Lundberg and Marynia Farnham had pointed out to any residual "female egalitarians" that

> for the male, sex involves an objective act of
> his doing but for the female it does not . . .
> her role is passive. It is not as easy as rolling off
> a log for her. It is easier. It is as easy as being
> the log itself.[14]

If there was widespread female frigidity, it was because modern woman suffered from "morbidly intense ego-strivings"; "rivalrous" feelings toward the male prevented her from attaining the passivity of a truly feminine woman, i.e., of a harp or a log.

So, almost necessarily, the area of maximum sexual preoccupation—the female orgasm—became a combat zone in the battle of the sexes. If the orgasm count was low, and everyone believed there was a national deficit of female orgasms, the blame could be apportioned either way. The man might be inadequate in his "performance" (though, with the weight or blame shifting toward women, specific male shortcomings, like premature ejaculation, were not yet major focuses of anxiety). More likely, in the prevailing judgment, the woman was frigid, or, in some deep way, withholding and resistant. Marriage, especially the ingrown, isolated marriage of the suburbs, provided a lifetime forum for mutual recrimination and resentment that could be deflected from the bedroom to the breakfast nook and back again.

On the eve of the sexual revolution, and prior to a developed feminist analysis of sexuality, there was no elucidation of America's orgasm impasse outside of psychoanalytic thought. In his introduction to the 1966 anthology *Psychoanalysis and Female Sexuality*, the prolific psychoanalytic commentator Hendrik M. Ruitenbeek offered an analysis that was curiously modern, even covertly feminist, in its focus on women's inferior social status. Along with Marie Bonaparte, Helene Deutsch, and other Freudian analysts of women's condition, he believed that true or mature female sexuality was passive and vaginally centered. Active, clitoral sexuality was immature and represented a refusal to accept the lack of a penis and "the male organic and psychical elements" that go with it. Thus, to grow up along psychoanalytically acceptable lines, "the active little girl must change into a far more passive creature." However, all kinds of complex changes, which Ruitenbeek associated with women's relative emancipation, had made "the female movement to passivity . . . more difficult in our time." In a remarkably perceptive passage, he explained how frigidity, or the failure to achieve fully passive, vaginal orgasm, was actually a "rebellion":

In a world where male activity sets the standards of worth—and analysts point out that both physiologically and psychologically, male sexual performance is an achievement—female experience in sex as in other aspects of life takes on the character of a peculiarly ambiguous struggle against male domination.[15]

The struggle was "ambiguous" because, in the Freudian scheme, there seemed to be no way to win. Ruitenbeek acknowledged that even psychoanalytically adjusted women might fall apart:

Some women submit; they do not rebel; they do not become aggressive and therefore a threat to the men in their lives, but their inability to enjoy their assigned role or to react against it leads to feelings of despair and to a kind of disintegration of the self.[16]

The woman who did have the spunk to "react," one way or another, was no less pathetic. There was no way to escape the passivity imposed by nature—without becoming a lesbian or other deviant, as Bonaparte cautioned in her contribution to Ruitenbeek's anthology. And there was obviously no way to "achieve" passivity by actively striving for it. All that Ruitenbeek could advise was that women scale down their expectations to more diffuse satisfactions than orgasm:

In my opinion, too many contemporary women tend to forget that satisfactory sexual experience entails something more than orgasm. Now as in the past, a woman can know sexual gratification by satisfying the component drives of her ego: awareness that she is desirable, ability to excite the man sexually, childbearing, and the aim-deflected pleasures of affection and tenderness.[17]

The "aim," Ruitenbeek implied, was still penetration and vaginal orgasm, but the contemporary woman might have to settle for cuddling.

SEX AND THE BIG CITY

If sex was stymied in the suburbs, a new terrain for erotic experience was opening up, by the early sixties, in the emerging "singles culture" of the cities. The cities had always lured young men and women from the monotony of rural life. By the mid-twentieth century, big cities were drawing young women from small cities; Jacqueline Susann "escaped" from Philadelphia to New York and the chance of an acting career in the late thirties. With the growth of corporate bureaucracies in the fifties, it was no longer only the daring or exceptional young woman who headed for the skylines after college or high school; thousands upon thousands of women were drawn in by the expansion of secretarial and clerical office jobs. In New York's Upper East Side, which was to become the first singles "ghetto," a real-estate boom in high-rise apartments and renovated tenements matched the in-migration of hopeful secretaries, stewardesses, editorial assistants, and would-be models and actresses marking time as receptionists or waitresses. Three or four "girls" might share a two bedroom apartment for three hundred dollars a month, losing some roommates to marriage, others to discouragement (there was usually a hometown to return to for the girl who failed to make her way), while all the time gaining new recruits from college campuses and small Mid-western cities.

The young middle-class woman who arrived in New York in the late fifties or early sixties probably expected to marry and retire to the suburbs in a few years, for the experts still agreed that "motherhood is the defining feature of a woman's life," but in the meantime she had sexual advantages—and possibilities—she would never regain as a housewife. First, she made her own money, so she was not required to "work" on a relationship out of sheer financial need. Like the fictional Anne Welles, she did not have to brood forever over a sexual disappointment; she could move on to a more satisfying partner. Second, she inhabited a social world that was infinitely richer in heterosexual contacts than the unisexual married women's world of shopping centers and playgrounds. There was the office—a work world which was mostly female and certainly male-dominated, but which offered opportunities for fantasy and flirtation. And there was the public space of streets, bars, even bookstores and buses, where a woman could move anonymously from one encounter with a potential partner to the next. As historian John d'Emilio has argued, the postwar cities—especially New York and San Francisco—provided the setting for the creation of a gay culture.[18] And for young, single, heterosexual women in the fifties and sixties, the city held forth an entirely new vision of female sexual possibility—and the first setting for a sexual revolution.

Other settings, too, fostered a rapid change in women's sexual expectations. On college campuses—which, like big city apartment complexes, offered a modicum of independence and a large population of young, single people—numerous studies documented a rapid decline, during the sixties, of the number of women who held on to their virginity until graduation. And although the sexual revolution was seen by many blacks as a white affair, *Ebony* noted in 1966 that it seemed to be having a profound effect on the young, middle-class black woman, who was "freed . . . from many inhibitions imposed on her by a now outdated puritanical outlook on sex . . . [and] like her white sister, has gained a new perspective on herself." *Ebony* attributed the change in part to the civil-rights movement, which had helped black women overcome the twin stereotypes of the Jezebel and the sexless Mammy and achieve "awareness of her true sexual self."[19] Whatever the sources, or the setting, a generation of young, mostly middle-class women were undertaking a sexual revolution or, at the very least, were being swept along by it.

The first spokeswoman for the revolution was a woman whom many feminists would be loath to claim as one of their own, but of the two best-sellers on women's condition—Helen Gurley Brown's *Sex and the Single Girl*, published in 1962, and *The Feminine Mystique*, published a year later—Brown's was in many ways the more radical. Friedan documented the discontents of middle-class housewives and proposed a "new life plan for women," which would include both motherhood and a career. Brown went further and announced that marriage was unnecessary and that a new life was already possible, the life of the single, urban, working "girl." Brown's book was a gushy guide to self-improvement, in the style she later immortalized in *Cosmopolitan,* while Friedan's was first-rate journalism. But it was *Sex and the Single Girl* that disposed of what Friedan called the feminine mystique in a few brief, confident sentences. "You may marry or you may not," she told her readers:

> In today's world that is no longer the big question for women. Those who glom onto men so that they can collapse with relief, spend the rest of their days shining up their status symbol and figure they never have to reach, stretch, learn, grow, face dragons or make a living again are the ones to be pitied. They, in my opinion, are the unfulfilled ones.[20]

Recall that Brown wrote this at a time when the *Ladies' Home Journal* still found most of its young readers looking ahead, not only to marriage but to the details of their future kitchen decor. Even the "new" urban, single women Brown addressed were still hoping, for the most part, that their stint in the city would culminate in an engagement and retreat to the married suburbs. Brown was way ahead of her time; the skirt-suited, full-time career woman, for example, would not emerge as a feminine role model until well into the seventies. But Brown was not so far ahead as to neglect the frustrations—and aspirations—of millions of very conventional and nonradical American women. Her book *Sex and the Single Girl* was a best-seller at a time when "feminism" did not even exist in the American political vocabulary, and when most middle-class women could imagine few options other than marriage and full-time motherhood.

Sex and the Single Girl argued simultaneously for women's financial independence and sexual liberation —a heavy burden, one might think, for such a lighthearted, chatty book. For Brown, though, the two goals were almost indistinguishable: Sex justified the need for financial independence, because the single working woman could spend money on the clothes and cosmetics and apartment accessories that would make her sexy; in fact, it was Brown's impression that she had more to spend "than any but a wealthily married few." Singleness itself was essential to sexiness, and not only because of the variety and availability it implied. Friedan found that housewives were bored; Brown announced that they were also boring, unattractive, and no match for the sexual challenge of the single girl:

> There is a more important truth that magazines never deal with, that single women are too brainwashed to admit, that married men *and* single men endorse in a body, and that is that the single woman, far from being a creature to be pitied and patronized, is emerging as the newest glamour girl of our times.[21]

What made the single woman sexually superior to women who had married? How could the erstwhile spinster meet the psychoanalytic criteria for feminine fulfillment? "She is engaging because she lives by her wits," Brown explained. "She supports herself." In contrast to the married woman, "she is not a parasite, a dependent, a scrounger, a sponger or a bum."

If single women were sexy, they also had a right to

sex, and perhaps the most important thing about *Sex and the Single Girl* was that it legitimized the sexual possibilities opening up to young, urban working women. Brown offered no new moral perspective on premarital sex, which was still viewed as a social problem and symptom of eroding values; she simply stated that it was happening, at least in cities large enough to accommodate the new breed of woman. Responding to articles in *Reader's Digest* and the *Ladies' Home Journal* advising single women to either marry or say no, Brown reported:

> I don't know about girls in Pleasantville and Philadelphia, where these magazines are published, but I do know that in Los Angeles, where I live, there is something else a girl can say and frequently does when a man "insists." And that is "yes." . . . Nice girls *do* have affairs, and they do not necessarily die of them![22]

This was, for many women in 1962, a major news item, almost as if a cure had been found for a fatal illness: "Nice" girls, meaning middle-class girls in pink- or white-collar jobs, not "sluts" or "whores," were having affairs and they were surviving. Sometimes, Brown acknowledged, they did get hurt and suffered, but happily "quite a few 'nice' single girls have affairs and do not suffer at all!" So extramarital sex did not have to mean ruin, as *Reader's Digest* warned, or be a sign of sickly obsession, as Friedan feared. Brown's single girl was not "using" sex to fill a void, as did some of the slatternly matrons described by Friedan; she had plenty of other things on her mind, like, Brown suggested, "retailing, advertising, motion pictures, exporting, shipbuilding." For a vibrant, self-determining single woman, sex was not a dangerous emotional morass but something to seek because you felt The Urge. With revolutionary simplicity, Brown explained that the number one reason for a single woman to start an affair was because "her body wants to."[23]

Within a few years after the publication of *Sex and the Single Girl*, the single, sexually acquisitive way of life for women would no longer require book-length vindication. By 1964, there were enough single girls (and envious married women) to warrant Helen Gurley Brown's transformation of the failing, family-oriented magazine *Cosmopolitan* into the *Cosmo* we know today. The first singles bars (Maxwell's Plum, P. J. Clarke's, T.G.I. Friday's) opened in Manhattan's Upper East Side, and new words entered the American vocabulary: "relationship," to accommodate both marriage and "affairs" (at the same time "affair," with its permanent image of marginalization, became archaic); "lifestyle," to accommodate singleness as well as marriage (and eventually homosexuality as another "alternative"); and "singles" itself as an adjective which might pertain to a neighborhood or a lifestyle. The commercialization of singles' needs—through bars, resorts, magazines, etc.—helped create a singles culture and identity which, over time, had less and less reason to feel defensive in the face of the married majority. In a 1969 book, *The Single Girl's Book: Making It in the Big City*, which could be taken for a pallid sequel to *Sex and the Single Girl*, Stanlee Miller Coy assumed that young women just want to know where the singles action is (in Chicago; the Near North Side, Old Town, and the Prairie Shores high-rise complex; in Boston; Beacon Hill,

Back Bay; and so forth through "those seven cities" offering outposts of singles culture). In New York, the new culture had long since achieved a critical mass, and "you can singles bar-hop up and down Third, Second, and First avenues on the Upper East Side, seeing thousands of singles."[24]

As the sixties wore on, the limitations of the new urban singles culture would become more and more apparent, even to its devotees. It was an all-white culture, largely untouched by the movements of the sixties, upper-middle-class in ambition, and conservative in all ways but sexual. The gap, for example, between New York's Upper East Side singles enclave and the center of Harlem's night life on 125th Street might have been forty miles instead of forty blocks, and the Lower East Side, which briefly supported a hippie culture second only to Haight-Ashbury's in San Francisco, might have been a foreign country, invisible from the subways rushing upscale singles from their apartments uptown to their jobs in the financial district. Within the singles scene, there was a gradual disenchantment with the ritual of sodden pickups, one-night stands, and the "meat-market" atmosphere of the bars. More sophisticated singles of both sexes began to settle in new territory (quickly gentrifying it, however, to their own tastes), to meet in therapy groups or events advertised in *The Village Voice*, and to look for opportunities for psychological "growth experiences" in their sexual encounters. But the singles culture, even at its most crass and preppie-conformist, nurtured women's sexual revolution: It *was* the mainstream, and in it casual sex was normal, acceptable, and in no way compromising to a woman's marital or career aspirations.

Unless, of course, she got pregnant; and in the sixties, with abortion still illegal, an accidental pregnancy was at best a costly and traumatic mishap. Though illegal, abortion was not unavailable, but an illegal abortion was likely to be exorbitantly expensive, horribly unsafe, or both. The birth control pill, which was a more reliable contraceptive than the diaphragm, reduced the chance of an unwanted pregnancy and gave many women the illusion of sexual invulnerability. But the pill was neither a necessary nor sufficient cause of women's sexual revolution: When the hazards of the pill became widely known in the late sixties, thanks in large part to Barbara Seaman's book *The Doctors' Case Against the Pill,* young women did not abandon the sexual revolution—they campaigned to legitimize abortion.

MASTERS & JOHNSON AND THE NEW SEXUAL MATERIALISM

The opportunities for more sex and sex with more men did not, at first, change the nature of the sexual experience itself for women. A single cosmopolite, no less than the long-term housewife, still faced the social definition of sex as intercourse and orgasm as the more or less spontaneous proof of womanhood. One woman, a college roommate of one of the authors, reports that as a young woman in Los Angeles in the early sixties, she had "about a dozen" lovers in three years, but

> my feeling for quite a while was that sex was
> no big deal. I had a girlfriend who claimed to

have ecstatic orgasms every time she went to bed with a man, so I naturally figured there was something wrong with me. . . . But with twenty years of hindsight I realize that it was just bad sex. The most sophisticated man I knew got all his information from D. H. Lawrence and Henry Miller, and the others had no information at all. Either way it was something that usually happened in the dark, that took fifteen minutes or less, and left me wanting to turn on the lights and read a book. It was not something I thought a lot about until I had to get an abortion in 1965, which cost over $500, and then I thought: Was it really worth it?

Sex and the Single Girl had said almost nothing about sex itself, and left the mysteries of the orgasm to the psychiatrists. Under the heading "You're Frigid," Brown advised:

> If after some experience you are still unable to enjoy making love, *and this bothers you*, psychiatric consultation may be in order.[25] (Emphasis added.)

Sex was still in the dark, and any problems that arose were in the minds of women, hence in the terrain of psychiatry.

It took the successors of Kinsey, William Masters and Virginia Johnson to turn on the lights and restore the human body—especially the female body—to the discourse on sexuality. What they established—about the female capacity for orgasm and the centrality of the clitoris to female sexuality—is by now well enough known. Less well known today is that none of this should have been news, even in 1966, when *The Human Sexual Response* was first published. Up until and for some time after Masters and Johnson's media triumph in the late sixties, most psychiatrists and psychoanalysts clung to Freud's theory of the female progression from immature clitoral sexuality to normal, mature vaginal sexuality, and postulated an exclusively vaginal orgasm for the successfully adjusted woman. But a wealth of contradictory evidence had been available for decades. There was the fact that the vagina has almost no nerve endings, while the clitoris is far more richly nerve-endowed than any part of the male sexual apparatus. There was Kinsey's documentation of the extent of female masturbation and lesbianism, practices which may have been "immature" by psychoanalytic standards but were apparently orgasmic. Reviewing the evidence, psychiatrist Judd Marmor had concluded in 1954 that clitoral sexuality persisted in adult women and that there was probably no such thing as a purely vaginal orgasm. By 1960, even the redoubtable Freudian Dr. Helene Deutsch publicly conceded her doubts about the existence of a psychoanalytically correct vaginal orgasm.[26] So if it was a surprise when the two St. Louis sex investigators revealed the intensity of clitoral sexuality and its role in female orgasm, it was only because of the psychiatric establishment's dogged adherence to the vaginal orgasm as prescribed by Freud.

Masters and Johnson employed a careful public relations strategy, designed both to keep them in the limelight and to maintain their aura of academic detachment. They offered scientific briefings for the press, but would not appear on television talk shows. They wrote an advice column for *Playboy*, but would not stoop to debate their critics. Between 1966 and 1970, articles about and occasionally by Masters and Johnson appeared in almost every mass circulation magazine, from *Redbook* to the *Saturday Review;* their book and a popularization by Ruth and Edward Brecher had become best-sellers. But it was not only skillful PR that made Masters and Johnson a household word, or, more accurately, an infallible bedroom reference. Their findings arrived at a time when expert theories of female sexuality ran increasingly counter to women's social experience. In psychoanalytic theory, female sexuality was an exercise in passivity, as complementary to male sexual activism as vagina to penis, and female orgasm was a magnificent surrender, symbolic of woman's acceptance of her subsidiary role in life. So for women, the official "meaning" of sex—the message emerging from all the sensations, positions, etc.—was powerlessness, and intercourse was an act of submission redeemed only by the certainty of a man's love. But if you were not married, or were tired of marriage, if you were self-supporting and adventurous, capable of sleeping with strangers or even social "inferiors," then sex had to "mean" something other than a submission to cosmic necessity. Masters and Johnson potentially offered a new social meaning for sex, one that was more consistent with women's emerging sense of independence.

The most common, and loudest, response to Masters and Johnson was that they had stripped sex of any meaning at all. The experiments, for many critics, were more shocking than the results. In a laboratory, Masters and Johnson had followed seven hundred volunteers (divided roughly evenly by gender) through various stages of arousal and orgasm, charting changes in the appearance of the genitalia, body motions, skin conductivity, etc. Some of the subjects were observed during heterosexual intercourse; others were studied while masturbating, either by hand or with artificial assistance. You had to wonder, the critics insisted, what kind of mind could have devised such an experiment, or, worse, what kind of person could be so depraved as to volunteer for it. Then, with the ad hominems out of the way, but before getting to the actual findings, there was the disturbing fact that there was anything to observe at all: that sex could occur in a laboratory, under the scrutiny of technicians, between strangers, or between people and vibrators, in a tangle of wires leading to monitoring machines. Liberal sociologist Kenneth Keniston complained that Masters and Johnson "repeatedly reduce human sexuality to physical responses," though, of course, only physical responses are accessible to quantitative measurement. Psychoanalyst Natalie Shainess railed that Masters and Johnson had released "a pipeline of pornographic sewage . . . into the vital heart of our life," corrupted youth, cheapened and "thingified sex," "trivialized it . . . [and] trampled on the ultimate mystery of life."[27] If sex were no longer the "ultimate mystery," it could mean anything —or nothing—like any sensation or any tracing on a laboratory recording device.

Finally, there were the findings themselves: that women actually had greater orgasmic capacity than men and were capable of multiple orgasms; that women have only one discernible kind of orgasm; and that it was more intense when self-induced by clitoral stimulation than when achieved through heterosexual intercourse. The implication was clear: Women did not need men for orgasmic sex. In fact, as Dr. Masters himself suggested, the presence of a partner could be a "distraction" to a woman on her way to orgasm. In an article in *Commentary*, Dr. Leslie Farber gleefully mocked Masters and Johnson for introducing the specter of the sexually self-sufficient woman:

> Her lust would lie to hand, ready to be invoked and consummated in sickness or in health, in coitus or "automanipulation," in homosexuality or heterosexuality, in exasperation or calm, hesitancy or certainty, playfulness or despair. . . . In other words, her sexuality would be wholly subject to her will.[28]

FEMINISM AND SEXUAL REVOLUTION

It was Dr. Farber's genius to anticipate almost precisely the feminist interpretation of Masters and Johnson. A psychoanalyst, he had written with the smug security of a man who knows feminism only as a diagnostic category. In the forties, Lundberg and Farnham, still eager to reduce women's sexual initiative to that of a log, had echoed the prevailing opinion on feminism. They described it only in the past tense, judging it to be "at its core a deep illness." "It was out of the disturbed libidinal organization of women" that accompanied "modern life," they wrote, "that the ideology of feminism arose."[29] Friedan had done her best to rehabilitate the

term, but it was only in the late sixties, on the crest of
the radical movements for peace and civil rights, that
large numbers of women dared to flout the Freudian
stigma attached to feminism and declare themselves a
radical movement of women and for women. One of
the earliest and most radical initiatives of these new
"radical feminists," as they called themselves, was in
the still confused and contradictory area of sexuality.

In taking up the issue of sex, the radical feminists
opened up entirely new terrain to political purview,
and in the process, redefined "politics" itself. To the
earlier, and now older, feminists like Friedan and the
National Organization for Women, which she had organized in 1966, women's rights were to be achieved in
the public realm of jobs, legislation, and conventional
pressure-group politics. The "private realm"—which
only the radicals conceptualized as an equal sphere of
female activity—was at best uninteresting, and at worst
a swamp of trivial and personal preoccupations. But to
the younger radicals, every repressed corner of private
life and daily experience—from housework to sexuality
and childbearing—was a valid arena for political action.
Consciousness-raising groups encouraged women to
trust their subjective experience, even when it contradicted male judgment or expert opinion. Sex—the area
of secrecy and self-doubt and of maximum competition
between women—was opened up to informal analysis
and sharing. Did you worry that you might be frigid?
Fake orgasms to please a boyfriend? Secretly prefer
masturbation, or wonder about lesbianism? So, it
turned out, did almost everyone else, and not every
woman could be as frigid or sexually warped as the
marriage manuals and therapists insisted. It did not

take long for women, buoyed with the confidence of the new movement, to trace the links connecting women's widespread sexual anxiety to their feelings of worthlessness and self-hate, and hence to the social oppression of women as a group.

Masters and Johnson's work was already widely known by 1968, the year the women's liberation movement announced its emergence. There is no way to know whether the early feminists would have dared to defy Freudian sexual dogma on the strength of subjective experience alone. Mainly by chance (though Virginia Johnson was in her own way a feminist), they did not have to: Here was a body of objective, and by most standards, respectably scientific findings on which to rest the case for a radically new, feminist interpretation of sexuality. The critics of Masters and Johnson had feared that sexual reductionism would lead to sexual nihilism. Reduced to anatomy and sensation, sex would lose its old meanings—love, commitment, and the established sex roles—and come to mean nothing at all. Feminism offered sex (as revealed by Masters and Johnson) an entirely new set of meanings. Sex did not have to be a microdrama of male dominance and female passivity; it was, properly understood and acted on, an affirmation of women's strength and independence.

"Think clitoris," concluded Alix Shulman in her 1971 essay "Organs and Orgasms," for if the vagina was the stronghold of Freudian, male-dominated sexuality, the clitoris was the first beachhead of feminist sexuality.[30] Some feminists, like Germaine Greer, criticized the early, exclusive championing of the clitoris, and later feminist work would expand the genital erotogenic area to include the entire vulva and perianal region.

But the first task of feminist sex rebels was to resurrect the long repressed—and sometimes even surgically excised—clitoris. It was visible proof of women's sexual autonomy from men, the possibility Dr. Farber had glimpsed and psychoanalytic theory had done so much to discredit. With Masters and Johnson's "discovery" of the clitoris and its central role in orgasm, it was possible to think of heterosexuality and even intercourse itself as an "institution," rather than a physiological necessity. In the 1970 essay "The Myth of the Vaginal Orgasm," Anne Koedt easily swept aside the old sexual dogma and spelled out the implications of clitorally-centered sexuality: If only for "strictly anatomical reasons," women might just as well seek pleasure from other women as from men. Koedt's classic essay was no less than a declaration of sexual independence; women could now be sexual, fully orgasmic beings not only outside of marriage but apart from men, who, she acknowledged, now had good reason to "fear that they will become sexually expendable."[31]

Feminists also seized on Masters and Johnson's other major finding—that women's orgasmic capacity far exceeded that of men. Dr. Mary Jane Sherfey's work, popularized in Barbara Seaman's *Free and Female*, argued that women, not men, were the sexually aggressive, orgasmically potent sex, capable of "having orgasms indefinitely if physical exhaustion did not intervene." Frigidity had been a social artifact of the vaginally centered sex men preferred; the clitorally aware woman was sexually voracious to the point of being a threat to the social order. Women's true sexual drive, Sherfey wrote, was "too strong, too susceptible to the fluctuating extremes of an impelling, aggressive eroticism to withstand the disciplined requirements of a settled family life."[32]

The feminist reclamation of sex made women's liberation, at least for a brief few years in the early seventies, as much a movement for sexual liberation. Clearly, women had been deprived, sexually stunted in service to the vaginal and phallocratic sex imposed by men. They needed more sex, but they needed sex in a variety that went far beyond the traditional in-and-out, man-on-top, intercourse. Clitoral sex, Alix Shulman pointed out, demanded a wider range of options, including oral sex, lesbian sex, and positions for intercourse that were more favorable to clitoral stimulation. All the old prohibitions and taboos would have to give way to the needs of the sexually liberated woman. Masturbation, for example, had been found by Masters and Johnson to produce the most intense orgasms in women, so feminists reclaimed it from the status of a "filthy habit" to a legitimate sexual alternative. At the high point of the fusion of feminism and sexual revolution, feminist conferences routinely offered workshops and consciousness-raising sessions on sexuality in general, genital and body awareness, and techniques of masturbation. Betty Dodson, a popular advocate of masturbation and leader of "bodysex" workshops, expressed the new feminist optimism about sex in a 1972 article in *Ms.:*

> Exploring my sexual potential has taken me on many paths of learning and change. Reclaiming my body as a source of strength and pleasure has given me power over my own life and the freedom to design my sex life creatively, just like painting a picture. Self-sexual-

ity, along with heterosexuality, homosexuality, bisexuality, and group sexuality is simply all part of human sexual behavior.[33]

But there was controversy from the beginning over the status of sexuality in the fledgling women's movement. Betty Friedan and others in the leadership of the National Organization for Women feared that the radical feminists' sexual heterodoxy—especially the encouragement of lesbianism—would marginalize the movement from the mainstream, which still consisted of married, presumably sexually orthodox, housewives. Others worried that sex was a detour leading to individual self-improvement and away from political involvement; certainly orgasms, now that the anatomy had been clarified, were easier to achieve than equality. But on the whole, feminism was strengthened by its appropriation of the sexual revolution. Sex *was* a major preoccupation for thousands of mainstream women locked in the orgasm impasse created by Freudian dogma, and for many of them, the feminist solution had the force of revelation. Books celebrating female sexuality—including *Our Bodies, Ourselves,* Seaman's *Free and Female* and many others—offered an instant boost in self-confidence as well as a lasting message about the dignity and value of women's experience. Instead of narrowing the movement to a subculture of politicized, urban women, sexual liberation contributed to the populist outreach that eventually brought the movement itself into the mainstream of American culture and politics. And, what is perhaps no less important, the sexual liberationist thrust of the movement protected it from the well-worn psychoanalytic slur linking feminism to frigidity and sundry deeper derangements of the libido. You could say, and many men did at first, that women became feminists because they were frustrated, or were too unattractive to find husbands. But you could *not* say, "All they need is a good lay." Feminists were doing very well in that department, thank you, and what they most emphatically did not want was a man's idea of quick and easy sex.

What feminism did for women's sexual revolution is a longer story, and one which we will see played out in succeeding chapters. Helen Gurley Brown's sexual revolution had stopped at the bedroom door, leaving any disappointments that lay behind it to the psychiatrists. Feminism opened the door, aired the room, and advanced the revolution into the smallest gesture and caress. Men's needs and women's needs were not automatically compatible, and the liberated woman had much more to say to a man than "Yes." As the psychoanalysts had suspected, heterosexual sex was a battleground in the war between the sexes. But victory was not what the psychoanalysts recommended: Real winners were conscious participants, fighting for what they wanted. If the battle seemed to men to rob sex of its "mystery," if the clitoris seemed like a demanding intruder, there was still no turning back. Feminism had used the sexual reductionism of Kinsey and Masters and Johnson to create a program of sexual reform, and too bad for the retrograde male who felt, like Norman Mailer,

> a hate for the legions of the vaginally frigid, out there now all the pent-up buzzing of a hive of bees, souped-up pent-up voltage of a clitoris ready to spring![34]

3
The Battle for Orgasm Equity
The Heterosexual Crisis of the Seventies

For men, the point of sexual revolution was, above all, more sex. If there was a problem, it was scarcity; and if there was a solution, it was greater quantity and availability. *Playboy*, which for most men represented *the* sexual revolution until women launched their own demands, rarely hinted at any qualitative transformation of sex itself. The centerfold models were selected to look as much as possible like the girl next door or down the hall in the typing pool; and the message, at the simplest level, was that she was much more available than you might have thought. Norman Mailer, for all his hostility, was one of the first to see that women had more in mind than "more." Women's sexual revolution meant that heterosexuality itself was about to be redefined.

As women's heightened expectations began to spread from the urban singles culture to the suburbs, the media responded with a sense of crisis. The divorce rate was rising precipitously, and it was clear that one of the biggest trouble spots was in the bedroom. For example, in 1972 *Life* singled out as a "typical" American couple David and Lynn Maxwell, who had been married for twelve years, had two children, and were now on the verge of divorce. In a feature article, the Maxwells went public with a list of problems, not the least of which was sex. Lynn asserted she could no longer sleep with David until she achieved more freedom in other areas of her life. "Before we were married David and I had a great sex life," Lynn said. "After we were married sex was one more obligation . . . making love was a very empty thing, and afterwards I would get so depressed."[1] Both had gone out and found alternative sexual partners. At least for Lynn, sex now signified everything that was wrong with their marriage.

David was angry that he was losing his traditional wife and baffled by what Lynn wanted from him. "A major friction which had readied David for his affair," *Life* reported, was Lynn's increasing involvement with women's liberation. David lived in fear that Lynn would actually become "confident and self-reliant," transforming not only their sex life but all their domestic affairs.

As women's sexual revolution spread to thousands of other "typical" American couples, the ancient, male question "What do women want?" began to take on distinctly sexual overtones. Did they want affection or technique, more cuddling and conversation or more decisive climaxes? And if women got what they wanted, what was in it for men? In the literature of male angst that has flowed prolifically since the beginnings of women's liberation, men tried out a variety of responses. Herb Goldberg, psychologist and men's liberation spokesman, tried to refocus attention on what he saw as the neglected penis, even claiming that men, when suitably aroused, were as capable as women of multiple orgasms. At the other extreme, the male lover of a well-known radical feminist announced that he now managed to have sex without erections, which seemed to him to be an atavistic reminder of male domination. A more typical response is represented by a recent book billed as a "survival guide" for men, which finds the aftermath of sexual revolution "frightening," and complains that "bedroom conversations focus on the female orgasm and performance evaluation [of the male]; the tender pillow talk is gone."[2]

A large part of the problem for men like David Maxwell was just that: There was so much *talk* about sex. Before the advent of women's sexual revolution, a man didn't have to worry that his wife would confide her sexual dissatisfactions to the press; in fact, he probably didn't suspect that there were any dissatisfactions to confide. Sex was part of a wife's responsibility; and if, as was frequently the case, it wasn't all that rewarding for her, any marriage counselor would have pointed out that bad sex was certainly not a justification for ending a marriage. In the paradoxical advice of the psychiatrists, women simply had to work harder to overcome their inability to relax and enjoy it. Prior to feminism and women's sexual revolution, wives kept silent about their sexual disappointments because they did not want to incriminate *themselves*.

There was a deeper problem. If men didn't know what was expected of them—or at least claimed to have no idea—it was because the heterosexual "act" itself was in the process of fundamental revision. Sex had meant intercourse, plus whatever preliminaries were required, by civility or affection, to achieve it. Now women were reporting that intercourse was incidental to their enjoyment; feminist writer Germaine Greer defined it as "masturbation in women's vaginas"—an embarrassing denouement for the premier event of the heterosexual relationship. Obviously homosexuals had done without vaginal intercourse, and, with the emergence of the gay liberation movement in 1969, it was apparent that gay sex was not—as had been commonly believed—a fumbling, pathetic substitute for the "real thing." So if heterosexual sex was not the spontaneous union of two physically complementary bodies, what *was* it?

But at the very moment, historically speaking, that the question could be raised, there were no longer any clear authorities to provide the answer. Women's sexual revolution, reinforced by the scientific rediscovery of clitoral sexuality, was rapidly discrediting the old medical authorities who had presided over sexual matters for at least a century. In the seventies there were no experts, or rather there were suddenly thousands of experts, each with a particular notion of how heterosexuality might be salvaged and reconstructed. The battle of the sexes, which had focused until now on the causes of female frigidity, now shifted to the question of "technique," or, more generally, *what was to be done.*

DEMEDICALIZED SEX

Before the sexual revolution, the public discourse on sex was dominated by the medical profession. Medical doctors—gynecologists and psychiatrists—wrote the popular guides to sex, chastely called "marriage manuals"; they appeared in magazines to answer anxious readers' questions; and they convened in academic gatherings to discuss sex, its failures (such as frigidity and impotence), and deviant forms. The medicalization of sex assured that there must be such a thing as "healthy sex", but by definition—and by way of defining it—healthy sex was ringed by its less than healthy, pathological variations. Doctors and the audience for their opinions were concerned with where to draw the line and how, if possible, to "treat" those who fell outside of it—the too avid, too slow, too specialized, too polymorphously promiscuous.

Any sex manual is inevitably a definition of sex: To describe "how to" is to define what there is to be done. The classic medical advice book *Ideal Marriage* stood out, not only for the largesse of physiological detail it provided but because it consciously, and painstakingly, undertook the problem of definition. Van de Velde offered what he believed was the "most exact and complete definition of normal sexual intercourse":

> That intercourse that comes between two sexually mature individuals of opposite sexes; which excludes cruelty and the use of artificial means for producing voluptuous sensations; which aims directly or indirectly at the consummation of sexual satisfaction, and which, having achieved a certain degree of stimula-

tion, concludes with the ejaculation—or emission—of semen into the vagina, at the nearly simultaneous culmination of sensation—or orgasm—of both partners.[3]

This definition, which was faithfully cited in later sex manuals such as Dr. Eustace Chesser's best-selling *Love Without Fear,* established not only what was normal or, more accurately, "ideal" but what the sex "act" was: preliminaries leading to vaginal penetration and ejaculation or, simply put; foreplay and intercourse. There could be many variations along the way. Van de Velde, for example, recommended the "genital kiss," a tentative version of oral sex, though how this was to be achieved he declined to explain, saying only that the technique could be "constructed" from a knowledge of "the kiss in general" and "the special structure of the female organs." For the most part, however, the road was straight and narrow. To meander off course or to fail to reach the destination ("nearly simultaneous . . . orgasm") was to jeopardize one's marriage, sanity, and physical health.

While the medical account of sex turned women into passive objects of male attention, it also gave them a powerful new way of perceiving their own sexual experiences. To Van de Velde, sex was a straight path leading to orgasm for both partners. This single-minded emphasis on the orgasm as the irreducible unit of sexual pleasure meant that if women had the right to pleasure within marriage, they also had the means to assess whether that right was being fulfilled. More to the point, if frigidity was as widespread as doctors suspected, women had a way of expressing the precise measure of their discontent. So it was ironic that the medical view of sex, which all but abolished women as active, conscious participants, also helped inspire the assertive new orgasm acquisitiveness that Betty Friedan noted, disapprovingly, among American women on the eve of the sexual revolution.

Medicine began to lose its authority over sex just as the sexual revolution began. For one thing, medicine had always deferred to psychoanalytic theory in matters of sex—hence the orgasm as an affirmation of adult married life, potential motherhood, and, in advanced versions of the theory, female masochism. But in the mass culture, psychoanalytic theory was now being forced aside by a more cheerful, open-ended outlook on the human condition. Humanistic (soon to be "popular") psychology valued "growth" itself above any presumed end point, such as marriage or parenthood. Instead of being a ratification of "marital adjustment" and female conformity, healthy sex could now be understood as a means to personal growth, hence by its nature not restricted to one position or sequence of acts, or even to one partner. In the postmedical vision of healthy sex offered by popular psychology, a varied and abundant sex life was the prerogative of any questing individual and, it was available, potentially, to anyone who was open to "growth".

Equally important to undermining medical authority was women's own changing experience of sex. The single most irrefutable measure we have of a "sexual revolution"—the vast increase in women's extra- and premarital experiences that occurred in the sixties and seventies—meant that tens of thousands of women were no longer viewing sex simply as a means of pushing a relationship closer to marriage but as a realm of experimentation and pleasure to be indulged in for its own sake. To young women in the mid-sixties, the shock troops of sexual revolution, the medical representation of sex as the touchstone of "marital adjustment" could only seem arcane, if not faintly repulsive. No wonder that the first feminist sallies into sexology—*The Hite Report* and *Our Bodies, Ourselves*—took women's own experience as the relevant data. In the seventies, more and more sex books would be authored, not by M.D.s and other "experts" but by ordinary people using everyday language.

With the medical monolith—foreplay plus intercourse—out of the way, the new "experts" began to redefine sex as a variety of options from which the savvy couple could pick and choose. The most significant "innovation" to enter the sexual mainstream in the seventies was oral sex—a possibility the medical sexologists had barely hinted at. Oral sex, of course, had always existed. Daring teenagers in the fifties tried "69"; and John Updike's 1960 best-seller, *Rabbit Run,* featured a shocking (though by today's standards, somewhat sketchy) incident of fellatio. Oral sex gained prominence in the seventies in part because of the increasing awareness of gay and lesbian sexual practices but also because it seemed to offer a solution to the crisis of heterosexual sex. Unlike intercourse, oral sex isolated the most sexually responsive organs—the clitoris and the penis—and dispensed with the relatively inert vagina. And unlike intercourse, oral sex seemed to offer the possibility of making heterosexual sex more reciprocal and egalitarian: Either partner could do it, and either could, presumably, enjoy it. For women, particularly "frigid" women, oral sex made orgasm possible, even probable.

But oral sex was not automatically reciprocal or even mutually pleasurable. In the sexual discourse of the seventies—which included not only sex manuals but surveys, confessional literature, and a new genre of couple-oriented pornography—oral sex was a contested zone. Men fantasized about unlimited fellatio; and, to judge from the pornography directed to them, were even beginning to prefer fellatio to vaginal penetration. Women—or women influenced by the new feminist views of sex—were looking to cunnilingus as the obvious way to satisfy clitoral sexuality. Who would get which, and in what amount, would become a subject for negotiation, debate, and no small amount of tension.

THE RISE OF ORAL SEX

"Now don't turn up your nose and make that ugly face" scolded J in *The Sensuous Woman*. "Oral sex is, for most people who give it a try, delicious."[4] In 1969 some readers were shocked—even appalled—by the frankness of this new sex manual. Oral sex was still not discussed openly and many people associated it with venereal disease. The outrageous and mysterious J reassured women that "kissing a man's penis [is] a lot more sanitary than kissing him on the mouth." Joan Terry Garrity was born in Minneapolis and moved to New York in 1960, where she worked for ten years as a book promoter. She used a pen name for her graphic best-seller because the average woman was not supposed to be voraciously interested in sex. (Garrity confessed much later to *People* that when her publisher revealed her true identity, she was primarily concerned about her mother's response to the book.) J displayed her knowledge of male genitalia and was proud of her expertise. Her enthusiasm helped sell nine million copies, and *The Sensuous Woman* is still in print.

The success of this manual was due to J's radical departure from mainstream sexual technique—and from popular ideas about women's attitude toward sex. Instead of a reverential attitude toward the male apparatus, she was breezy, witty, iconoclastic. All this from an "ordinary" person—a woman no less—without a medical degree. *The Sensuous Woman* had no scientific pretense nor any information culled from the medical profession to justify its personal perspective. This was straight talk for women, unfettered by academic jargon, geared to those who were just entering the sexual arena or needed a refresher course to update their technique. Sex was defined primarily as a physical, rather than an emotional, act that could be performed by any two people, regardless of whether they were married to each other. J offered some basic skills that anyone could learn easily enough and, unlike male experts, she conveyed her appreciation for the opposite sex: She liked men, and found no particular deep meaning in sex—other than pleasure.

Garrity described her own pet techniques in a language that middle-class housewives could easily understand. She personalized her methods by assigning them names that made sex sound as ordinary as cleaning house: "The Hoover requires using your mouth like a vacuum cleaner." Fellatio, performed in a number of original styles, dominates Garrity's sexual act. For in-

stance, "The Butterfly Flic," another one of her cre-
ations, required locating the corona and carefully using
"your tongue [to] flip it lightly back and forth . . . like
you were strumming a banjo." Immersing herself in
parts of the anatomy that her male peers ironically had
left unattended, J recommended sucking on testicles—
and even more: "When your man reaches that final
peak, he could decide to come in your mouth. Did I
shock you again? Yes, this is another completely normal
sex act." On the brighter side, she informed her readers, "It's also pretty hard to get pregnant this way."

J's practical attitude toward sex and her everyday
language turned her predecessors into dinosaurs by
comparison. But like the majority of manuals prior to
The Sensuous Woman, this one was also extremely phal-
locentric. She assumed women were typically nonorgasmic, and that this condition could be lived with—for
better or worse. A chapter called "Orgasm—Yours, Not
His" is devoted to faking orgasms: "To avoid disap-
pointing him and spoiling his plateau of excitement and
sexiness . . . fake that orgasm! Throw in a few extra
wriggles and a yelp or two along the way to match his
passion—but be careful not to ham it up too much."

Although J had never been swept away by the feminist rebellion, she was arming the troops for the sexual
revolution. Garrity wasn't interested in questions of
gender or sex roles; nevertheless she defined sex as an
arena that women could control, where they could explore a number of different options. Even married
women who were sexually frustrated were free to sleep
with other men (affairs with their husbands' friends
were more advisable than picking up men on the
streets). J's realm of sexual possibilities included swap-

ping and orgies ("If you go don't wear a good dress") and even anal sex ("Cheer up," she comforted her stunned readers, "this is an optional").

In *The Sensuous Woman* sexual variety outside the boundaries of traditional monogamy is considered fairly mundane, indicating a growing female wanderlust. But J knew that fellatio was still a problem for women, single or married, who were beginning to broaden their sexual horizons. For men, fellatio was fast, could be performed almost anywhere, and required no birth control. For women, there was no automatic appeal. They not only had to get used to the idea, but fellatio was a difficult physical proposition. One woman in particular, Linda Lovelace, the star of the porn film *Deep Throat*, exemplified this female dilemma. By working to overcome the gag reflex, she became renowned for her dubious skill. The film articulated contemporary problems with oral sex (obviously from the male point of view) and picked up a cult following: *Deep Throat* became a vehicle for the mass (male) fantasy of oral sex.

Even though this was a typical porn film (characterized primarily by a low budget, inexperienced actors, and a minimal story line that interrupts long sex scenes), it was one of the first "couples" or "crossover" films to engage a mixed audience of men and women. Lovelace became a cult figure because of her sexual dexterity, bringing pornography out of its male ghetto. In the film, she plays a visiting nurse who cures men's "illnesses" with a miraculous throat that seems to have no end. One of the many climaxes in the film occurs when a doctor discovers why Lovelace gets so much pleasure from her work. As he pokes around inside her

mouth he discovers that instead of tonsils, she has a
clitoris in her throat. "It's not so bad," the doctor reassures Lovelace as she bursts into tears. "You should be
glad you have a clitoris at all."

In a sense the doctor was right. The average woman
in a porn film (let alone real life) had no clitoris: It was
rarely given any screen time and was never the source
of any kind of sexual excitement. Geared to the male
spectator, these films were not interested in pleasure
from a woman's point of view, and oral sex was never a
reciprocal act. But in *Deep Throat* the clitoris is the
center of attention, the key to a woman's sexuality—
and, as usual, extremely difficult to find.

In real life, however, Lovelace wasn't getting any
pleasure and what she was swallowing was largely her
own pride. In *Ordeal,* her autobiography, she tells the
story of her marriage to porn pimp Chuck Traynor,
whom she credits as her fellatio mentor. At his instiga-
tion, Lovelace practiced opening up her throat during
oral sex—bypassing her tonsils—until this expertise became her trademark. According to Lovelace, one of
Traynor's favorite pastimes was to put her into a trance
and give her posthypnotic tasks to perform. One evening after putting her under he ordered her to wake
up, perform fellatio and simultaneously have an orgasm. Lovelace put on such a good act that Traynor
used the evening's entertainment as the basis for *Deep
Throat.*

Lovelace eventually got up the courage to leave
Traynor, who, she explained, had forced her to be a
slave to his sexual and economic interests. She eventually changed her name, remarried, and discovered
God, all to the media's delight. But Traynor's brutality

never showed up on film, and even if it had, *Deep Throat* might still have become a classic. For men, it was wishful thinking to rediscover the clitoris in the throat. But by the early seventies there was more than enough evidence that the significance of this small, elusive organ could no longer be underestimated: The clitoris wasn't a figment of the female—or feminist—imagination. *Deep Throat* accurately expressed the male anxiety about integrating the clitoris into sexual practice. Men, it seemed, longed for the clitoris to be a moveable feast.

ORGASM EQUITY

By 1975 a *Playboy* study found that 90 percent of married women under twenty-five had integrated fellatio into their regular sexual agenda. Even *Redbook,* whose readers were supposedly more interested in interior decorating and cooking than sex, discovered that of 100,000 women surveyed that same year, 85 percent of them indulged in fellatio.[5] "While a certain feminist fringe may have found a target in the male genitalia, by far the vast majority of us like penises," wrote Chris Weygandt in *Oui.* Arguing against the feminist notion that women had to become much less subservient to the phallus—at least in bed—Weygandt scoffed at the idea that women's sensibilities "were offended at the mention of oral sex."

But when a *Oui* survey in 1980 asked women who *didn't* like fellatio, "Is the prime difference in your attitude that he doesn't reciprocate?" 75 percent replied yes.[6] "My ex-husband was wild about blow-jobs," wrote one of the women, "but he hated going down on me. So what was the point of giving him special treatment? He didn't make it worth my while."[7] For heterosexual women, making sex reciprocal required a major transformation of the sexual act. But oral sex was still a better battlefield than traditional intercourse—if only because it was, after all, potentially reciprocal.

During the seventies even mainstream porn magazines were beginning to discover the clitoris. "Stimulating a woman's genitals with a penis is like trying to cut a diamond with a chain saw," wrote the author of a letter to one such publication.[8] Yet in the early seventies, both Kinsey and Morton Hunt, the author of *Sexual Behavior in the 1970's,* found that on the average only 56 percent of men surveyed found cunnilingus desirable. A typical woman reader wrote to one porn magazine as late as 1980 to complain that a third of the men she was meeting "wouldn't do it for a million bucks" and another third "act like they're doing me this big favor." The figures went up to 74 percent toward the end of the decade, but that statistic seemed too high when compared to the revelations of *The Hite Report.* In 1976 Shere Hite's study indicated that only 42 percent of the women she surveyed were reaching orgasm through oral stimulation of the clitoris. But the number could have been greater with a change of male perspective: "Most oral stimulation was done for arousal, not orgasm. All too often cunnilingus was offered by the partner for very short intervals."[9]

But *The Hite Report* went further than simply arguing that women wanted more oral sex. For the first time, a volume of female voices statistically turned women's right to good sex into a political issue. The question of how to have sex could not be reduced to technique. "If we make it easy and pleasurable for men to have an orgasm, and don't have one ourselves, aren't we just 'servicing' men?" Hite asked her readers. She demonstrated statistically that more women were able to orgasm on their own than with men, who mostly encouraged them to be passive and obedient in bed. "If we *know* how to have orgasms, but are unable to make this a part of the sexual relationship with another person, then we are not in control of *choosing* whether or not we have an orgasm." Hite's analysis concluded that women, when it came to sex, were "powerless."

This feminist analysis of heterosexual relations immediately provided more grist for the sexual revolution. And when it was published in 1976, Hite's controversial study was backed up by the liberal medical establishment. Citing Masters and Johnson, Kinsey, Seymour Fisher,[10] Helen Kaplan,[11] and a burgeoning movement of sexologists, the evidence was conclusive that frigidity was not a female problem: Many heterosexuals were unable—or unwilling—to have good sex. "It is difficult to believe that the millions of otherwise responsive women who do not have coital orgasms," Kaplan asserted, "are all 'sick.'" Women weren't sick, Hite passionately argued and scientifically demonstrated. They were oppressed by men, whose definition of intercourse left them cold. When one woman in *The Hite Report* was asked whether her partners were even aware of her orgasms she answered: "Usually not. Sometimes they ask, and sometimes they assume I [have one] or else they couldn't care less."

The Hite Report put pressure on men who couldn't "care less." Hite's study was a call to action for women to openly demand orgasmic sex. Many of the women in her book clearly articulated what was wrong with sex down to the last anatomical detail. Women, it seemed, could speak about sex, and now it was time for them to speak to men. Hite stripped the orgasm of its layers of patriarchal illusions, and powerfully enhanced a woman's ability to negotiate in bed.

THE JOY OF SEX

If there is a single metaphor for the reconstructed heterosexuality of the seventies, it would be a bartering session. Since all pleasures were not mutual or simultaneous, equity would have to be achieved through a conscious process of give and take. The ideal setting would be a long-term relationship, with plenty of time for negotiation and reassessment. If this seemed like a cold and unromantic approach—especially to men—it was still the only practical way for women to assert their needs. In the imagination, though, it transformed sex from a magical communion to the kind of social interaction one might experience in the business world or, for that matter, a garage sale.

The Joy of Sex, published in 1972, could be described as the ultimate postmedical sex manual. There was no longer one definition of sex, only an array of options to choose from—like goods in a department store or dishes in a lavish buffet. The author, Alex Comfort, was a doctor, but that was almost incidental to his sexological pursuits. Although he became a household name in America only at the age of fifty-four, he was already well known in his native England as an "anarcho-pacificist philosopher." An antiwar activist who refused to serve in World War II, a Cambridge scholar, poet, novelist, husband, father, and gerontologist, Comfort was not the kind of man one would have expected to write a best-seller on sex. Yet in England his long-standing interest in these matters was public. A nudist and member of the Diogenes naturalist club, Comfort sought out situations where he could observe sexual behavior. After moving from England to Santa Barbara in the early seventies, he frequented the Sandstone Retreat in Topanga Canyon. This fifteen-acre estate was a commune for those interested in "liberated" sexual encounters. There were rules that governed membership to the club, but sexual freedom was the highest priority. "Often the nude biologist Dr. Alex Comfort," reports Gay Talese in *Thy Neighbor's Wife,* "brandishing a cigar, traipsed through the room between prone bodies with the professional air of a lepidopterist strolling through the fields waving a butterfly net." Comfort "brought a bedside manner to an orgy," and unlike other professionals, he even participated: "After he had deposited his cigar in a safe place—he would join a friendly clutch of bodies and contribute to the merriment."[12]

Comfort preferred the immediacy of actual human behavior to lab work. Hugh Kenner speculated in the New York *Times* that this might have had something to do with the fact that his scientific curiosity had led him to experiment with gunpowder at the age of fourteen and blow away most of his left hand. This disaster didn't prevent him from getting a Ph.D. in biochemistry, or completing ten books by the age of twenty-four. For the most part, however, he remained outside of the lab. By

American medical standards, this was a radical practice. To Comfort, the problem with medical experts—and their manuals—was their obsession with everything other than what people actually *do* in bed. He blamed his peers for treating the average person like a sexual cripple who used a manual as a crutch, rather than a guide to creative possibilities.

The Joy of Sex was more of a "manifesto," to use Comfort's term, than a medical tract, and it implicitly took the medical profession to task. Instead of narrowing the definition of sex to determine normalcy, Comfort offered an encyclopedia of sexual acts that gave credibility to any form of experimentation. *Joy* mocked the experts who had made sex taboo, and people guilt-stricken for enjoying themselves. "There is nothing to be afraid of and never was," he concluded in *More Joy,* his sequel. "We [the experts] manufacture our own nonsense."

Joy was written for men and women, whom Comfort assumed were equal players in sex, although at times his masculine bias showed through. Structuring the manual like a cookbook was an ingenious way to illustrate his notion that people may have very different kinds of tastes, but, it was to be hoped, they all had a sense of humor. Variety, for Comfort, was the spice of life: "Being stuck rigidly with one sexual technique usually means anxiety," he wrote in his introduction. In Comfort's opinion, sexual intercourse was vastly overrated by his peers, who organized their manuals around one position in which the penis could most successfully penetrate the vagina. *Joy* was filled with sexual techniques ranging from the mundane to the exotic. His intent was to help people heighten their sexual experiences by exploring a variety of techniques, rather than perfecting only one. Comfort did not ask his readers to search for one monumental, ever-elusive orgasm. Instead he encouraged both men and women to go out and explore a new limitless sexual landscape which his book described in graphic detail—without setting up any rules or regulations. Reading *Joy* was the closest thing to an uncensored tour of a sexual paraphernalia shop.

The book implicitly redefined heterosexuality as a pluralist institution that could accommodate those who chose the monogamous heterosexual path—which Comfort acknowledged as the main highway and often the safest route—and those who detoured through bisexuality, which he considered perfectly normal. "In threesomes and group experiences, which are getting more acceptable socially," Comfort told his readers, "'bisexual' opportunities are inevitable." Even more unusual in a mainstream sex manual, Comfort theorized: "All people are bisexual. . . . If it worries you don't do it, but it isn't bad magic, poisonous or odd."[13]

There was no "correct" way to have sex in *Joy,* which included some extremely idiosyncratic techniques. In a section called "Sauces and Pickles" he covered obscure practices like "femoral intercourse," a technique used to maintain a woman's virginity without contraception: "The woman presses her thighs together and the penis goes between them with the shaft between her labia. This gives the woman special sensations—sometimes keener than penetration—so it's well worth trying." Comfort included technical information for virgins on the one hand and sophisticated sadomasochists on the other. The use of chains was on the menu for heterosexuals: "Women like both the coldness and the symbolism," he opined, "while men can spend hours locking and unlocking them," along with "discipline," the code word "for beating each other." Erogenous zones covered the body from top to bottom, including "big toes." For those who were curious, Comfort recommended pornography, leather, sexual substitutes, and more. Essentially anything was worth a try between consenting adults.

What distinguished this poet/scientist from his predecessors was not only his encyclopedic scope but the illustrations he used to accompany his text. While the jacket of the book was snow white, the inside title page had a drawing of a naked man and woman rolling into position for oral sex; on the following page, they are casually enjoying cunnilingus. (At the time one male reviewer attacked Comfort for having fallen prey to clitoral emphasis and downplaying fellatio.) Readers became familiar with this nameless, imaginary couple, who popped up on almost every page, trying out dozens of techniques. They were symbolic representations of the sexually liberated generation; the man sported a scruffy beard; the woman, armpit hair. Relaxed and uninhibited, these erotic illustrations were a long way from the anatomical drawings in conventional manuals that highlighted one part of the body or another—without giving away the whole picture. In a separate color signature titled "The Art of Making Love," the *Joy of Sex* couple is carefully drawn in sequence, going through all the motions.

In addition to these illustrations, Comfort used art to make a connection between sex and the imagination. In a most surprising section, he included a series of full color, erotic Japanese prints. These were pictures that could potentially turn his readers on or, at the very least, stir the imagination. It was an intellectual's peep show that managed to parody the entire genre of sex manuals. Manuals of course were rarely illustrated at all, to keep them fit for the library shelf. Some future authors found it so difficult to compete that they resorted, like Dr. Ron Pion in *The Last Sexual Manual*, to recommending that heterosexual couples buy two copies of *Joy*—his and hers—go through and rate each sexual technique, and then trade copies. At the time it seemed that Comfort had written the last word on sex —it was difficult to imagine going any further.

SEXUAL FANTASIES: THE MENU EXPANDS

"Admittedly the reader will at times have to fight off shock, prurient interest and distaste," wrote J in an introduction to *My Secret Garden*. "This is no coffee-table book."[14] In 1973, one year after *The Joy of Sex*, Nancy Friday's first sex manual was advertised as a "milestone in sex education." While Comfort was promoting the notion of heterosexual variation, Friday was out doing fieldwork on women's sexual fantasy lives. The result was a range of sexual possibilities that went well beyond Comfort's generous menu. *Publishers Weekly* commented that Friday was "astonishingly outspoken, even in a period of unusual sexual frankness." But men had been frank about their fantasies—not women. Friday's work was shocking because women had remained outside this aspect of the public discourse on sex.

My Secret Garden was filled with hundreds of wild fantasies illustrating how easily women could imagine themselves with aggressive sexual lives. Friday stressed that an active imagination didn't necessarily signify sexual problems; many women fantasized during masturbation, or while they were having perfectly adequate sex. No one, it seemed, wanted to act their fantasies out in real life—that would come later. But to the distress of many readers, the female libido was shown to be remarkably similar to that of the male; women were interested in adulterous affairs, incest, prostitution, voyeurism, S/M, rape—even sex with animals. By traditional standards, this was the landscape of *male* sexual lust.

The book was riddled with complaints about husbands who were either unwilling or unable to satisfy their wives. Consequently some women fantasized about sex with each other: "My husband doesn't know about my secret desire to sleep with another woman," a middle-aged woman confessed. Friday devoted an entire section of *My Secret Garden* to such fantasies involving "Other Women." Most of her subjects had never had a lesbian experience, yet they relied primarily on same-sex fantasies while having sex with men or masturbating. "I enjoy a full sex life with my husband. Sometimes, however, I do have lesbian fantasies. . . . I am not a lesbian in any way—I enjoy men too much—but when it's necessary for me to masturbate . . . While my boyfriend is making love to me I often fantasize about my best friend. . . . Does this mean I'm a latent homosexual?"

Most modern experts might have answered yes, but if Friday's book was prophetic in any way, it signaled the homosexualization of heterosexual sex. The similarities between these once distinct groups were now becoming visible in sexual fantasies and popular notions of sexual practice. The newfound appreciation of oral sex was not so new to the lesbian community. And, as monogamous relations broke down, single women were no longer necessarily looking for a permanent male date. The homosexual delight in sex as a defiant expression of liberation was catching on with heterosexual women.

My Secret Garden was so successful that Friday wrote two more fantasy collections. Like a feminist version of Hugh Hefner, she developed a market for a particular style of female porn. Although it was quite distinct from the male genre—written by and for women—much of the language was the same. "I would be joining the very army of inhibitors if I latinized my writing and drew a sharp line between my text and the four-letter-word language of fantasy itself." No one could accuse Friday of exploiting one sex to benefit the other, yet her books, like other forms of mass-market pornography, could as easily be used for masturbation as sexual edification.

Collections of women's personal experiences such as *The Hite Report* and *My Secret Garden* were now the vanguard of the genre. Friday was not predominantly interested in changing the social or sexual relations between men and women, but she, like Hite, gave the female subject ample room to speak. For women, it was the first time that a mass market was developing to actually solicit, digest, and eventually serve up their sexual desires to be transformed back into practice.

Comfort, Friday, Hite, et al. signaled the death of the medical profession's monopoly on sex. Any expert unable to shake the Freudian search for the exemplary vaginal orgasm seemed as rigid as the missionary position. Sex had been redefined as a social interaction rather than a hazardous undertaking that could only be discussed lying down on the couch. It was no longer a diagnostic test for female illness but a potentially orgasmic activity in which everyone had equal rights.

Now that the consensus around the definition of sex had crumbled, there was no one sex manual dominating the market as Van de Velde's had. The democratization of information made room for a cacophony of voices. Anyone who had anything to say on the subject regardless of credentials or ideological perspective found room to speak. In general, manuals that exclusively promoted monogamous sex were in the minority and most authors turned their attention toward the long-neglected female orgasm. That orgasm was now the subject of great debate, open to many different interpretations. Some authors treated it with spiritual reverence, others as an ordinary biological function—as mundane as digesting food.

Feminist psychiatrist Lonnie Barbach attempted to unravel the mysteries of achieving an orgasm by teaching women how to satisfy themselves. A self-described expert on masturbation, she advised nonorgasmic women to educate themselves in her techniques rather than count on male partners to lead the way to ecstasy. Barbach pointed out that even for heterosexual couples, the penis wasn't necessary for a female orgasm. (Neither, of course, was the vagina always useful to men.) "If the old thrusting in and out would do it," one of her patients at long last realized, "it would have happened by now."[15] In Barbach's manual *For Yourself,* the first step for women was spending some time alone to learn about their bodies. By 1975, masturbation wasn't news. Regardless, the word was considered too dangerous for prime time. Barbach had trouble promoting her book, as she was prevented from describing exactly what it was about.

Five years later when she published her sequel, *For Each Other*, masturbation was a household word. The average manual now included a section on female masturbation, offering a creative array of equipment that ranged from cucumbers to Coke bottles. But these techniques obviously didn't solve many of the problems between heterosexuals. Eva Margolies went so far as to suggest in *Sensual Pleasure* that sex with some men was essentially hopeless—no matter how well women knew their own bodies: "A small, but significant minority of men are only interested in their own pleasure." Margolies used to think that women should stay in their place and "grit their teeth," but during the sexual revolution she had a change of heart: "I've come to believe that such behavior is inexcusable, and unless you feel your physical well-being is in jeopardy, I suggest you get dressed and head straight for the door."[16] If a man was selfish, changing his personality structure was a job for the psychoanalytic profession, not a lover. The guiding principle throughout *Sensual Pleasure* was that sex had to be defined as a balance of power: "It's not fair to expect something of your partner without being willing to reciprocate." She had no illusions about mutual orgasms: Men and women would have to patiently take their turns.

SEPARATE BUT EQUAL

This new notion of separate but equal orgasms was displacing the old obsession with coming together. The experts had consumed themselves with methods to hold men back or speed women along. But getting into a rhythm to reach a simultaneous plateau was proved to be physiologically difficult. Sex was becoming more like jogging: It was better at one's own pace.

On the one hand, the female libido that had been revealed to the public at large had great similarities to its male counterpart. Yet, when it came to the pursuit of sexual desire, men and women were physically far apart. It wasn't simply a problem of mutual timing, but more basic than that, the mutual dependence of the penis and vagina was no longer the key for women, or even men, to sensual pleasure. Men and women, it seemed, had different styles and sexual tastes that could actually interfere with sexual relations. Whereas once heterosexuality had been thought of as "natural," almost automatic, men and women had discovered that their distinct sexual needs could actually get in the way of good sex. It was unrealistic to expect that either sex knew instinctively how to satisfy the other. Ending up in bed with a new partner was often a whole new exploration, rather than a familiar routine. "For the first time in my life," Ben, a thirty-five-year-old artist in New York, confessed, "I took a woman who obviously wanted to sleep with me home from a party to my loft. But she wanted me to perform certain acts in a particular way that I wasn't prepared for. I was so stunned, neither of us enjoyed the sexual experience and she went home in the middle of the night. I couldn't handle it."

How to Make Love to a Man by Alexandra Penny, expressed, more than any other manual, the growing physical alienation between heterosexuals. It was so difficult for men and women to satisfy each other simultaneously that Penny advised them to take turns, not during the same evening but alternately, with the woman giving the man whatever he wants one night and the man reciprocating on a separate occasion. Rather than refashion sex by bartering and trading sexual pleasures, Penny told her readers to get everything they want on *their* night. She advised women to take over the responsibility for sex, to conceptualize it ahead of time and aggressively go out and seduce the objects of their desires. The total experience required a major investment in the tools of the trade—makeup, new hair styles, sexy clothes, and gadgets—in order to pull off a professional act. This was theatrical sex, so tightly scripted that there was little room for spontaneous heterosexual impulses to destroy a scene.

The Penny method of making love to a man would have confounded Van de Velde. Her approach to sex acknowledged mounting heterosexual antagonisms based on the distinct sexual preferences of men and women. In the wake of women's sexual revolution, there was nothing "natural" about heterosexual sex, at least nothing more natural than masturbation, homosexual love, or any other "option." The old romantic model of sex as an experience of abandonment and self-loss would not work for a heterosexual world in which men and women stood so far apart in understanding each other's sexual needs. Sex was now something a

woman went into with her eyes open—figuratively at
least—her intellect alert, and her skills honed. There
was no reason a determined heterosexual woman
should not find as much pleasure as she was capable of
experiencing. But she had to negotiate, to bargain, and,
if necessary, to shop around.

If it still didn't work, other options were opening up
—ones which would have less and less to do with the
initial feminist impulse that inspired women's sexual
revolution. The crisis in heterosexuality had introduced
new metaphors for sex that drew on the world of market relationships: Sex as a system of bartering, sex as
consumerism. In the next phase of the sexual revolution, the metaphors would become reality. Women's
sexual revolution would be drawn into the commercial
marketplace; and women would be able to purchase
the means to sexual pleasure as impersonally as they
might expand their wardrobes.

4

The Lust Frontier

From Tupperware to Sadomasochism

On a muggy summer evening in a suburb of Washington, D.C., Jane Cooper kicked her husband and kids out of the house. Thanks to the 90-degree weather and Indiana Jones, they were far from unhappy spending the evening in an air-conditioned theater. Cooper didn't really mind the heat. It added some body to her limp brown hair and with a little suntan she could easily dispense with a layer of makeup. In the summer Cooper felt more relaxed. It was unusually quiet in her kitchen now as she emptied the ice into a container and refilled the trays at the sink. Tonight she was hosting a special event—a party for women only.

The doorbell rang and Cooper's stomach tightened. The guest of honor this evening was a door-to-door saleswoman with a trunkful of sexual paraphernalia, and the other guests were a group of Cooper's closest friends. In this neighborhood, vibrators in the bedroom were already as common as blenders in the kitchen, and Cooper's friends were interested in taking the next step: a private introduction to a broad range of sexual objects—from erotic lingerie to ankle restraints.

Women like Jane Cooper were lured into the sexual consumer market by offers of monumental orgasms requiring very little effort from either partner: creams promising to turn women into "savagely erotic and uninhibited" creatures; french ticklers guaranteeing "feverishly hot sex in seconds." If Jane's friends were searching for a new sexual thrill, they could browse through catalogs filled with Vice Spice Pills, Sta-Erect Sheaths, adult videos, and Emotion Lotions, to name only a few of the items. By making so many erotic products available, the consumer culture was encouraging her to play around, or at the very least to experiment with the purchase of an erotic product.

Home parties, as they are innocuously called in this small industry, are a popular way for women both to purchase sexual paraphernalia and bring an expert on sex into their living rooms. Tupperware-style parties where sexual aids are sold rather than plastic containers are no longer rare. Several businesses—some of which are owned by women—are now scattered across the country. Compared to shopping in a sex paraphernalia shop, a party offers a less commercial, more social context for imagining new sexual frontiers. For Cooper, organizing this party felt similar to doing community work. She was used to orchestrating block parties and car pools, but this was much more exciting—even a little secretive. Over the past few years "The Phil Donahue Show" and its parade of swingers, sadomasochists, male prostitutes, and other sexual mavericks had monopolized the conversation at many neighborhood events. Now they were after a live show.

Not so long ago the most common, and in most places the only sexual aid available to women was a vibrator packaged as an electric massager for a stiff neck. As long as the sole source of information on sex was the medical and pseudo-medical experts, and as long as they promoted intercourse as the only legitimate form of sex, sexual paraphernalia were nowhere to be found because they were simply unnecessary. There was nothing compelling to market, buy, or sell. But when sex became more varied than intercourse, new products emerged to complement an expanding list of sexual practices. Suddenly vibrators were not alone in the classified sections of pulp magazines but were accompanied by magic creams and edible nighties.

As women transformed sexual practices to meet their needs, they were quickly targeted as a new consumer class for the sex industry. There was nothing novel about dildos or the ancient Japanese tradition of ben-wa balls. What was new was the proliferation of objects and information for sale carefully aimed at women as the prime audience. In this consumer arena female sexuality functioned differently than it had previously in mainstream society: It was clearly unattached to reproduction, motherhood, monogamy—even heterosexuality. Women, whether gay or straight, married or single, all had something in common in this arena: The pursuit of pleasure—at a reasonable price.

Jane Cooper was surprised at how quickly her friends discovered that sexual paraphernalia were not obscene but playful and provocative—fruit-flavored creams and lotions were best-sellers. When a variety of vibrators were laid out on the coffee table, a discussion began on the idiosyncrasies of clitoral stimulation. Some women demanded strokes before intercourse, some during. One woman explained that her husband had to climax first for her to enjoy manual, oral, or any kind of sex. There was no formula offered that evening for "good" sex. In a sexual arena that promoted diversity, the "expert" had been replaced by a pluralist market, and purchasing power, rather than psychiatric insight or pseudo-medical information, was the key to an exciting sex life.

Indeed any object purchased and integrated into the sexual act brings with it a new sexual consciousness. The diaphragm, the first object that many women had to slip into their sex routines, was initially awkward. But experts advised eroticizing the process, turning the placement of birth control devices into sexual play. Sexual paraphernalia initially piggybacked on a birth control market offering flavored condoms and vaginal creams. But the range of products quickly outgrew their functional relationship to reproduction. Novelty itself held out the possibility of transforming the sexual experience—for better or worse—particularly for women whose monogamous sex lives had grown stale and routine over the years.

Feminism had helped to develop this new sexual arena by promoting masturbation and vibrators as keys to women's sexual independence. But it took American free enterprise to transform the search for sexual novelty into a small industry. In 1971, when two men opened a shop in New York City to sell water beds— clearly to enhance sex—business was slow. When the Pleasure Chest, as they called the store, added "amorous and prurient paraphernalia: lotions, cock rings, handcuffs, and dildos" according to a history printed in their catalog, business suddenly took off.[1] Today the Pleasure Chest is a multimillion-dollar operation with stores in seven major cities, a home-party division, and a huge mail-order department that sells hundreds of items.

The financial success of the chain was only made possible by diversifying its products to attract female consumers, who initially accounted for no more than 10 percent of sales. When the New York store originally experimented with a female window display in 1975, it was nervously greeted with a few giggles, according to Stan Farwell, who has been in the business for more than ten years. But the real goal was to turn women into serious consumers rather than window-shoppers, and this required some new interior decoration. "Pornographic" images of penetration were taken off the walls; the floors were carpeted and the store was bathed in pink lights. After six years and an active marketing strategy, 30 percent of the clientele was female.

"The changes were due to women's demands," said Farwell, which in part was true. Women—single or married, gay or straight—were more than happy to turn dildos and lotions into best-sellers. Today, the mail-order department receives about 500 orders a day for one item alone, a natural lubricant called "Foreplay," which rivals Baskin and Robbins in its variety of flavors. By 1983 more than half the customers shopping in the Pleasure Chest were women.

SEX IN THE MARKETPLACE

There had always been a sexual marketplace for men, offering pornography, prostitutes, strippers, go-go dancers, and more exotic possibilities for the connoisseur. The extension of the commercial sex industry to include women as consumers is, from a strictly egalitarian point of view, long overdue. As a setting for learning about sex, the marketplace offers some clear advantages over friends, medical experts, or even the more liberated manuals. The marketplace is impersonal; if there is a demand for something, it will sooner or later turn up, no matter how offensive it may be to some people's tastes. And the marketplace is democratic; its potential pleasures are not limited to the beautiful or fit, but to any woman who can shop.

In fact in some ways the market is especially congenial to women, given women's legacy of being made to feel sexually inadequate. The woman who consults a sex expert—even one of the more permissive radio personalities—or who goes to a bookstore to buy the latest published promise of "Great Sex!" is admitting she may not be sophisticated enough, experienced enough, or possibly *good* enough. But the woman who can enter the marketplace and shop for new sexual possibilities is in the familiar position of judging whether the merchandise is good enough for *her.* One of the reasons for the popularity of parties like Jane Cooper's is that they transpose the still anxiety-ridden subject of sex into one of the most comfortable and familiar settings of female domestic culture. Seated around a living room, comparing wares and experiences, the women are in charge—

only the products and the possibilities they represent are being judged.

The marketplace for sexual products, images, and even new forms of pornography for the female consumer has spread the sexual revolution to women who would never have attended a feminist conference on sexuality or perhaps even have read one of the new sex manuals. Home parties might seem laughable or peculiar to an urban sexual sophisticate, but to a woman in, say, suburban Ohio, they may be a major source of sexual information—packaged in a uniquely palatable form. For example, we were surprised to meet a young woman who is working her way through graduate school in psychology by giving home parties in rural Missouri. Weren't her wares a little racy for the Bible Belt, we asked. No, she insisted. "I get mothers and daughters, sisters—almost whole families—coming out to the parties together. There is a real fascination and the way we meet, in someone's home, is a very safe environment for finding out what you might want to know. And it's fun, too; it can get pretty raucous sometimes."

But if the sexual marketplace is impersonal, nonjudgmental, and pluralistic, it still has its own built-in biases. These biases are covert—invisible in a snapshot impression—and they have more to do with the nature of markets than the nature of sex. The market for consumer goods of any kind is ever-changing, quick to absorb each new novelty and abandon the old. We are barraged with fads—Smurf figures and designer jeans one year, videogames and oversize T-shirts the next. The minute we are jaded with one product or motif, the next one arrives; and each, of course, is temporarily a necessity. Without novelty and variety, short-term "necessities" and quick-turnover "classics," our consumer culture would go into decline and, so too, no doubt, would our particular variety of capitalism.

Even the nascent marketplace for sexual products both requires and generates variety. If sex were still what it had been in the marriage manuals of the fifties, there would be little or nothing to market. Even the now-staid and familiar vibrator would have no place in a sexual culture that denied the validity and autonomy of clitoral sexuality; flavored ointments would have no function in a culture that officially disapproved of oral sex. Sex itself had to undergo the diversification of the sexual revolution before it lent itself to being packaged and marketed in a form that women could consume.

Once sexual possibilities have been commoditized as products and aids, the search for novelty takes on a life of its own. If flavored creams are exiting one year, they will be old hat the next; what is daring the first time is soon routine. So if parties like Cooper's or stores like the Pleasure Chest are to draw their customers back, something new must be found to market. It is not a sign of moral breakdown or "excessive" permissiveness that the sexuality visible in the consumer culture seems always to be outreaching old limits: This is the dynamic of the market, and in sex as well as fashion or entertainment, it pushes always and inexorably toward new frontiers.

Thus the sexual marketplace both democratizes and *institutionalizes* the sexual revolution. Practices that were once pioneered by a few brave souls become, through the marketplace, the potential property of anyone. The variety once enjoyed by an avant-garde or urban elite becomes available through mail-order catalogs to a housewife in Iowa. The perverse becomes the commonplace. And as soon as it does, the market must reach further into forbidden areas for the next novelty, the next marketable sensation. In this way, the sexual revolution begins to take on a dynamic of its own, without conscious iconoclasm or risk-taking on anyone's part, driven along by the impersonal energy of the marketplace.

PORNOGRAPHY—FOR WOMEN?

The most visible—and perhaps the most innocuous—form of the new female sexual consumerism is the male strip joint, which by the mid-seventies had almost surpassed bowling as the most popular way to spend "ladies' night out." Male strip joints offer an experience of complete role reversal and a chance for grown women to shriek like teenagers and be as bawdy—at least verbally—as middle-aged swingers. If the role reversal allows the release of certain covert hostility to men—as some shocked male observers have guessed—it doesn't seem to bother the typical male performer. When a Washington *Post* reporter asked Michael Rapp, a dancer from Chippendales, a well-known club on the East and West coasts, what his parents thought of his line of work, he affectionately replied, "My mother comes to watch and my father wishes he could do it."[2] For women who enjoy the shows and use them to celebrate everything from engagements to promotions, it's clear that sexual entertainment doesn't have to involve sexual exploitation. Ironically, they have been more

than willing to learn how to objectify the opposite sex.
Strip joints offer groups of women a night out on the
town without their husbands—some of whom thoroughly approve of the phenomenon: "I encourage my
wife to go out with her friends to the clubs," a man told
his less liberated peers in a men's magazine. "When she
comes home at night we always have incredible sex."

By late 1985, male strippers had become an acceptable, almost routine part of female consumer culture.
In the film *Twice in a Lifetime,* a shy, middle-aged
woman who has been abandoned by her husband for
another woman is taken out by her daughters to a male
strip joint to celebrate her birthday, her new hair style,
and her recovery from heartbreak. It is impossible not
to be moved as the heroine, played by Ellen Burstyn,
emerges from her depression and begins to gasp and
giggle along with her daughters at the display of wrig-
gling male pelvises. The impact of the scene is distinctly feminist: Men are not such a big deal after all. In
fact, reduced to bikini shorts while dancing around to a
disco beat, they're fun to watch, and a little silly, too.

There is a similar message at the "male entertainer"
parties set at a Long Island health and diet spa for
women. On occasional Thursday evenings, rum and
Diet Coke is served after the last aerobics class, and the
forty or so participants, still wearing their sweaty leo-
tards, sit in a semicircle on the floor while the male
entertainer struts and strips. It is a neat symbolic re-
venge for the women, who have spent the last hour
confronting their own, never quite adequate bodies. In
the real world, these women know they will be judged
by their thick thighs or sagging bellies; in fact, a poster
on the wall shows a collage of gorgeous female torsos,

with the legend, "This is your competition." But on party night at the spa, it is the male who must exert himself, who must entertain and be judged.

The male stripper could be seen as a diminished version of the male rock star: Like the star, he is something for women to consume collectively; almost all the pleasure is in the group experience. No one, after all, goes to a male strip joint alone, without a contingent of friends to giggle and shriek with, just as a solitary fan is not likely to experience the transports of hysteria. But with the stripper, women have more obvious kinds of collective power than they do as a crowd of fans. The stripper is of course not a celebrity. He has no name or only a first name; he usually shares the stage with one or two other strippers; even the music, which was the excuse for the star's performance, has been reduced to a beat to drive the male pelvis. And what is perhaps most important—it is up to the women to tip the stripper. In a parody of male behavior, women clutch at his bikini and pull it open to tuck a folded bill inside. Thus is the phallus—the awesome centerpiece of fifties sexuality—demystified in the sexual marketplace.

Male strippers were only one sign of the growing female market for sexual imagery. By the late seventies, another formerly male sexual commodity—pornography—was being revamped for a female market. Ideally, viewing sex in all its varieties could be thrilling, even educational, for either sex. For women this was a novel activity, since images created for them, rather than men, were all too rare. But traditional pornography had objectified women to such an extent that from the point of view of the female spectator the content was either distasteful or excruciatingly dull. In particular, the women depicted in films were usually devoid of personality, and used mostly as physical receptacles for showers of sperm. This was a medium for men to enjoy with men, not with women, whose point of view had never even been a consideration.

In Hollywood, the film industry began to recognize the new female sexual consumerism of the late seventies with a succession of "hunks," actors who were often short on talent but long on muscle and sex appeal. Men were redesigned as sex symbols, a category previously reserved for the 36-26-34 female. Richard Gere, who played a rapist in *Looking for Mr. Goodbar,* turned up as the ideal male sexual commodity in *American Gigolo,* where his torso was seductively uncovered. In that film, he plays a high-class prostitute who takes particular pride in his ability to give women extraordinary orgasms. In *An Officer and a Gentleman,* which was notable for its steamy sex scenes, Gere's naked body actually flashed across the screen—unusual for an R-rated film. Gere hit the cover of *Newsweek* in 1983, as Hollywood's male idols became a national preoccupation for women. Another hunk, John Travolta, who danced to stardom in *Saturday Night Fever,* confessed in *Rolling Stone* that his biggest problem was getting a woman to treat him "as a person rather than a stud." Nevertheless, his ideal date had a "big sexual appetite" and needed no "coaching."[3]

The traditional porn-movie industry has also been turning its sights on the female market. "Combat-zone" theaters are making a stab at respectability by cleaning up their floors and their language: "Pornography" is passé and "erotica" is in. According to Ron Sullivan, the Eastern vice president of the Adult Film Association of

America, the key to bringing women in is "running erotic films in clean and well-lighted theaters complete with soft drinks and popcorn." But the rise of cable television, which allows anyone to watch X-rated films in the privacy of their homes, is unquestionably the best way to reach a female audience. By 1982 there were roughly 3 million videocassette recorders plugged into televisions across the country, and 22 million households were wired for cable TV; a selection of 200 adult entertainment stations was available in different parts of the country, which the industry claimed accounted for more than half the cable market.

By the mid-seventies, "crossover" films that had escaped the porn ghetto, like *Behind The Green Door* or *Deep Throat,* were becoming more visible. In 1982 *Roommates,* a typical crossover film, was so successful in New York City that it ran in a legitimate theater and received serious reviews. "I can't say *Roommates* is sexually progressive," wrote Carrie Rickey in *The Village Voice.*[4] But what made it worthy of note at all was the film's atypical attitude toward both sexes: Rickey called *Roommates* a "virulent man-hating document." It wasn't exactly for the raincoat crowd. The protagonists were women—not men—and many of the heterosexual sex scenes were shot from the female's vantage point. The film tells the story of three women who have active but very unsatisfactory sex lives. As they search for long-term (more traditional) relationships that offer recreational rather than abusive sex, we watch them wade through a selection of callous, women-hating, manipulative men. The message is that most men are evil, and that women have to search long and hard for any kind of decent sex at all.

"Erotica for women isn't flooding the market" wrote
Jean Callahan in *Playgirl*, "but it's on its way."[5] In an
interview with Callahan, Richard Pachenco, a popular
male actor in the X-rated market, explained the conscious changes that producers were attempting in order to attract a female audience: "Instead of seven out
of seven sex scenes being brutal and exploitative, only
one will be. The sex is more real. You'll still see arbitrary
fucking scenes—it's a shotgun blast meant to attract
everyone." Pachenco is best-known for his award-win-
ning performance in *Nothing to Hide* (porn "Oscars"
are given out by the Adult Film Association of America), where he plays a character who is made to look
foolish—almost retarded—because he doesn't want to
rape and exploit the opposite sex. But eventually he
meets a virgin whom he hotly pursues all the way to the
altar—a rare narrative development for a porn film.
"As more people [i.e. women] watch these films at
home," Pachenco predicts, "they'll get better. The bedroom is the environment in which adult films will become adult, instead of portraying a male sexuality arrested at the age of 13."

Meanwhile, the pornographic press was also reaching
out to a female market. Like cable TV, it had the potential to reach masses of women in relative privacy. *Penthouse* eventually gave birth to *Forum*, a porn publication that included articles oriented toward women. The
same size as *Reader's Digest* and *TV Guide*, *Forum*
could easily be purchased in drugstores or supermar-
kets and slipped into a purse. Unlike men's "skin" magazines, *Forum* didn't feature nude pinups of women as
sex objects but more often matched articles with softer,
"erotic" illustrations. *Forum* refused to tell us whether

their circulation is going up or down, but in October 1985 their print run was 598,000.

Small format porn magazines seeking a couples audience multiplied on the stands. While *Forum* includes nonfiction articles on sexually related topics along with letters from readers, *Penthouse* also offers its readers a more lurid magazine called *Variations*. Devoted exclusively to first-person narratives describing almost every sexual experience imaginable, *Variations* is raunchy. The editor, V. K. McCarty, who is referred to in the industry as "the grandmother of kinky sex," insists that all the letters are genuine. Unlike the more discreet *Forum*, *Variations* offers photographs of men and women in all sorts of strenuous poses, but McCarty believes the magazine is something "any American housewife would find palatable." As women began to show up in their rising circulation figures, the business department told editorial to "soften the graphicness of the sexuality." McCarty took "bare nipples off the cover" and dropped "incest and bestiality" from the magazine's pluralist menu of sexual dishes.

Perhaps surprisingly, S/M was one form of sex that *Variations* didn't have to drop in order to broaden its circulation. The editor herself was a notorious "dominatrice," a female expert in sexual dominance, who had told all in a 1982 article in *Penthouse* called "S/M for Beginners." A year earlier, *Variations* had already devoted an issue exclusively to the subject; it included articles on bondage, female domination, female submission, humiliation, the gay leather scene, branding and more. It contained detailed descriptions of almost everything anyone ever wanted to know about S/M, ostensibly from the mouths of typical married women:

> My husband and I have been married seven
> years. We have two small children and live a
> middle-class life in California. . . . The first
> time we actually tried B&D [bondage and dis-
> cipline] I tied my husband spread eagle on the
> bed and strapped him in a few times with one
> of his belts. It wasn't much, really, but I'll
> never forget how exciting it was to see for the
> first time, my husband helplessly bound, na-
> ked and under my control. Now . . . we have
> an interesting assortment of collars, whips,
> cock rings and other "tools of the trade."

Women counseled one another not to accept automatically the masochist's role unless by choice: "At first it
was difficult for me to get into the S/M scene because I
hate to be tied up," a frustrated female sadist wrote to
the magazine. "After a talk with my husband, however,
I found out that he had no objection to bondage. . . .
Today, in the dominant role, I have come to love our
S/M sessions." Dominant women even get rewards outside the boundaries of sex: "[Thanks to S/M] I've come
to enjoy being the complete boss," explained an anony-
mous reader, "and I leave lots of housework for Ned to
do!"

S/M ENTERS THE MAINSTREAM

The crowd at Jane Cooper's house had unanimously
negative responses to certain objects; they all found a
baby's pacifier in the shape of a penis repulsive—even
perverse. But its inclusion in the display didn't discour-

age anyone from participating in the party. In fact it was comforting to be able to draw the line somewhere by rejecting some products in order to heartily endorse others.

As the wine flowed, Cooper's guests examined Passion Flowers, Rub-Her Bands, Lick-Ness Monsters, erection and nipple creams, anal intruders, satin sheets, and Orgy Butter. When it seemed as if every imaginable item was out of the closet, the expert asked if anyone was interested in S/M toys. "If you're not," she seductively added, "it may be because you haven't seen what I have to offer." Despite a few groans, as the group anticipated the sting of her whip, everyone was curious about this part of the show. Instead of torture equipment, however, they were confronted with soft black leather ropes that are used to tie a lover down in bed. As the ropes were cautiously passed around, some women asked questions about bondage. But not everyone was a total novice.

"We were roughhousing one night after a lot of brandy," began Jill McLoughlin, as the crowd at Cooper's house quieted down. "Tom was on top of me, holding my arms down with each hand, while I had him in a scissors grip with my legs. He suddenly reached for a pair of stockings and managed to tie my arms to the bedposts. Then he pinned down my legs. We were laughing, biting each other—like kids—it was all very playful, very spontaneous. But I found myself tied down, unable to free my hands or legs. The last thing I was was angry or scared. My strongest desire at that moment was to surrender—give in totally to the sexual experience. I was in a frenzy and Tom was thrilled, not having gotten me as excited since our premarital days of heavy petting. Sex once again felt almost taboo." Jill and her husband had not repeated the experience, but for her it was a night to remember.

After two women purchase leather ropes ($34 a pair), it's time to go home. To Jane and her friends, S/M is no longer beyond the pale; it's something they expect to see—at least in attenuated form—in mainstream magazines, rock videos, and the fashion world. In 1977 when *Vogue* first published Chris Von Wangeheim's infamous photographs of Dobermans snapping at a model's ankles, most readers were shocked. Likewise, appalled critics questioned the use of S/M as a background for Geoffrey Beene's "metallic sandals" and "sliding necklines." This was pornography disguised as chic, high-fashion photography. The protest only underlined the power of the images, which seem to have affected American culture like a long-lasting aphrodisiac. On some level the connection between women's captivity, submission, and high fashion made sense, and S/M began to be a recurrent, if usually covert theme in fashion and advertising for women.

By 1981 S/M was no longer covert. In *Self,* Michael Korda, the editor in chief of Simon & Schuster, ascribed to the work of Helmut Newton, perhaps the most well-known photographer to create a context for S/M in high fashion, an "elegance with a flair for startling, sadistic sexuality."[6] Any reader who picked up this issue could have turned to the centerfold and mistakenly thought he or she had purchased a porn magazine: A double-spread color photo of a half-naked woman screaming in ecstasy as she receives a hard spank from a fully dressed man. Korda's article, "Love Bites and Slaps: What to Make of Them, When to Play the Fantasy Game, When to Draw the Line," described and endorsed the escalation of aggression in heterosexual sex.

Coming from Korda, the surgeon general of publishing, this was strong medicine for those who felt they had unhealthy sex lives. Pain, he argued, helped to intensify sexual pleasure. The caption accompanying the centerfold provided most of the evidence: "A sudden affectionate swat on the rear—one of love's traditional plays—usually elicits a response of shocked pleasure." For Korda, S/M was not only an accepted form of sex, it was even glamorous. He speculated that in a consensual situation, S/M was an opportunity for "a return, however momentary, to the animal self within each of us." Korda made S/M sound like an exotic drink that wasn't appropriate every night, but that could on occasion hold out the possibility of a new kind of sexual peak. Like homosexuality or marijuana, it took some time to get used to the idea, but S/M was easily packaged as a safe heterosexual sport.

There was actually nothing new about S/M, other than its visibility in the mass culture. Historians believe that S/M has been practiced since the Renaissance, although the medical community has only begun, with some anxiety, to explore the phenomenon. In a 1972 study of 141 suburban, married housewives, Dr. E. Hariton found that 49 percent of the women had submissive sexual fantasies.[7] Masters and Johnson completed a comparative study of the sexual fantasies of heterosexuals and homosexuals in 1979, in which they found that "forced sexual encounters" were prevalent fantasies for men and women, regardless of their sexuality.[8] Commenting on the study to the New York

Times, Bernard Apfelbaum, director of the Berkeley Sex Therapy Group, said, "It's important to look at the content of a sex fantasy during lovemaking for what it suggests about what's missing in the sexual encounter."[9] While the study did not indicate that men or women, regardless of their sexual preference, wanted to bring their fantasies to life, it did reveal that for many people, S/M was a typical erotic fantasy theme.

Statistically, too, there is evidence that S/M is entering "normal" sexual practice. As early as 1953, the Kinsey Institute found "sizable portions of their samples" had been involved in light S/M such as biting or slapping. More recently, in a study of a "self-defined" S/M group of 225 men and women, Dr. Charles Moser of the Institute for Advanced Study of Human Sexuality found "no evidence to suggest that the psychological functioning of the S/M self-identified individual was impaired." The majority of his sample rejected the notion that S/M was "inborn" (an animal instinct as Korda has suggested) or a "mental illness," and more than 45 percent found " 'straight sex' as satisfying as, or more satisfying than S/M," indicating that this population was not obsessively limited to one kind of sex.[10]

But it was the sexual marketplace, more than anything else, that brought S/M into the mainstream of sexual options. The market demands novelty, and by the eighties oral sex was no longer novel. It had been described meticulously in sex manuals, portrayed in the new "couples" porn, and promoted implicitly by the flavored cremes and ointments. Movie scenes suggestive of oral sex, or scenes of couples seemingly on the brink of oral sex, had become so routine that they barely warranted a PG rating. Little references to oral sex, like the bumper sticker recommending that one "Sit on a Happy Face," were hard to avoid and no longer shocking. The sexual marketplace needed a new frontier and by the eighties the only imaginable remaining novelty—perhaps even the last frontier—was sadomasochism.

S/M is not only the latest sexual novelty, it is perhaps the ultimately commercial form of sex. First, it lends itself to a more gripping form of imagery and presentation than any other activity can. In pornography based on oral sex, the creative challenge was to wrap some sort of plot around the various episodes of fellatio and cunnilingus. Oral sex is only an act, but S/M is itself a *drama*. There is no single act that defines it, only a drawn-out sequence of events that may in themselves not even be overtly sexual. The thrill is in the buildup; the "foreplay" is the play itself. So even in one of the most primitive and familiar forms of commercialized sex—the vignette presented as a letter to the editor of a porn magazine—S/M has much greater possibilities than any particular sexual practice. Anything else needs some crude narrative buildup: "She entered the room. I could see she was wearing nothing under the trench coat . . ." S/M, appropriately ritualized, contains its own narrative.

S/M has another, equally powerful, commercial quality: It is innately fetishistic; it *requires* paraphernalia. More familiar sexual practices might be enhanced with oils or cremes or eroticized birth control devices, but basically the human body is adequate for their performance. Hands, mouths, genitals, are "equipment" enough, and anything else—to touch, smell, or read as an adjunct to sex—is an aesthetic sidelight to the main event. The commercial possibilities are inherently limited.

Not so with S/M, which depends on an inventory of devices—whips, chains, ropes, even outlandish costumes. The gear is not just an optional enhancement, it is essential to the act—if not to the very imagining of it. Perhaps Van de Velde, the classic sex expert of the pre–sexual-revolution era, understood this when he defined "normal sex" as excluding "cruelty and the use of artificial means." The cruelty, even in its more harmless, ritualized forms, is hard to imagine without the devices; and the devices are hard to look at without imagining cruelty or at least the simulation of cruelty. If it is to be anything beyond routine brutality, S/M requires its collection of evocative objects. And if it is to be fresh and interesting time after time, its performance requires new objects—more horrifying bondage gear, more fetishistic outfits—to center the drama on. S/M almost requires a sexual marketplace, impersonally promoting the "objects" of desire. From a strictly capitalist viewpoint, it is the ideal sexual practice.

S/M owes its entrance into the sexual mainstream to its paraphernalia: The symbols and gear precede the actual practice into the homes and imaginations of millions. Thus a rock video on television can convey the possibility of S/M without being in any way overtly pornographic—simply through the images and gear. For example, a 1984 video by the popular group Duran Duran showed nothing suggestive of sex (we are tempted to say "normal" sex), but contained almost subliminal images of female figures in chains. Even the twelve-year-old viewers could understand that the reference was to "S and M," rather than to sex as we ordinarily understand it. Similarly it is the paraphernalia that brought S/M into the forefront of possibilities for the women gathered at Jane Cooper's home party. Introduced in the form of commodities, with prices and even sizes, S/M was no longer bizarre and disgusting— just something else for the curious consumer to try.

Certainly, women like Jane Cooper seem to be perfectly capable of experimenting with S/M without radically transforming their entire sex lives or becoming in any other way eccentric. While Cooper was the first woman on her block to host a home party, she is hardly viewed as a sexual maverick. Neither are any of her friends—secretaries, computer technicians, clerks, bank tellers—who are for the most part happily married women. For those of them who were having S/M fantasies, the home party provided evidence that they weren't alone, and no longer had to feel guilty. The consumer culture was offering them validation by selling items that could bring their fantasies to life. S/M had become visible.

THE DAUGHTERS OF DE SADE

While some women were experimenting with bondage or spanking, others were involved in a more extreme, ritualized form of S/M. For them S/M ironically provided the answer to a difficult question: How can men and women—gay or straight—play fair in bed? S/M could be a carefully constructed sexual ritual offering an enormous amount of control to both participants. For heterosexual women who desired more control over the sexual act—a common enough request—S/M offered a method of binding each partner to play by a set of mutually agreed on rules. The element of power —and powerlessness—inherent in the traditional heterosexual experience is the core of the S/M ritual. Dominance and submission, two roles most often played out in bed, are complementary elements in an S/M drama. For some men and women it is desirable to define these roles in order for each person to choose their favorite part.

Unlike the days before the sexual revolution, heterosexual S/M does not automatically assign roles based on traditional notions of gender. Men don't have to lead; or women, follow. Either sex can be dominant or submissive. "Leadership"—who does what first, when, and why—has always been an issue, particularly for heterosexuals battling for equality in bed. But for sadists and masochists, power is not exclusively located in the person directing the scene. To S/M devotees, there is no social value or inherent investment in either of these roles—which are mutually dependent and freely chosen.

The imagination is what shapes an S/M scene to meet the individual desires of both players. The top and bottom (as the sadist and masochist are called, respectively) often begin by familiarizing each other with their sexual fantasies; they choose one that is mutually pleasing to act out and then determine what equipment will be used and the limits of the scene. Often the bottom is given a code word that can be used to stop any particular act, while preserving the illusion that the sex is nonconsensual. While the roles of top and bottom remain rigid, it takes a great deal of communication prior to having any sex to determine the content of an S/M scene.

Given the openness—and confusion—over sex during the seventies, part of the appeal of S/M for some of its devotees was the rigid structure that it provided. If heterosexual women had difficulty getting men to perform, or even explaining what they wanted, here was one form of sex that could do away with the confusion surrounding the issue of equality in bed. Instead of kicking power relations out of the bedroom, as many feminists had recommended, sadists and masochists prefer to eroticize domination and submission. The issue of power, its use and abuse, creates the erotic content in a scene. The illusion that sex is not consensual empowers the top and turns the bottom on. Costumes are used to reinforce the notion that each partner is giving a performance and to authenticate the particular fantasy. In its most exaggerated form S/M is tragicomic theater: power here equals powerlessness.

"The successful S/M act can be compared to the successful production of a drama composed by two or more authors," said Terry Kolb, co-founder of the Till Eulenspiegel Society. "A great deal of intuition, ability to improvise, and cooperation is needed." This S/M society in New York City (named after a masochistic character in German folklore who preferred to climb up hills rather than down) began in 1976 and had three hundred dues-paying members by 1984. The purpose of the group is to support and educate the S/M community. "I was the only woman when we first started T.E.S.," secretary-treasurer Goldie told us (she does not use her own name in S/M circles to protect her job). "Now one third of the members are women." The

group offers Monday night lectures "on things like water sports, the history of S/M, or the perils of masochism." They are open to the public for a three-dollar
admission ticket.

The majority of members in T.E.S., according to
Goldie, are heterosexual submissives. "Most of the men
are submissive, while among the women it's about half
and half." Inside the S/M culture no one is surprised
that men prefer to be dominated by women. "If I had a
dollar for every man who asked me to switch, I'd be
rich!" reported Goldie, who has been a masochist for
the past thirteen years. In the S/M configuration, the
sadist is burdened with the responsibility for directing a
scene, turning sex into little more than a spectator
sport. The top must continually watch and gauge the
level of the bottom's sexual enjoyment in order to make
sure that no one gets hurt. While it is taboo to go beyond the predetermined limits of a scene, an experienced top stays close to the edge.

Insiders consistently report that masochists—male
and female—make up the majority of the S/M population. "It's a lot of work to be a good dominant," explains
Goldie. "You have to set the scene and all that. People
are lazy. It's easier just to be done to." Dominance,
once an honorable, male tradition, is now not a particularly desirable role to either sex. Dominants are so
much in demand that a new category called "masochist
servers" has developed to meet the need. These are
people who, though not usually dominant, are occasionally willing to perform certain acts. Apart from any
deeper psychological reason, masochism seems to be
more attractive because it's more rewarding. Paradoxi-
cally, the passive masochist is always the center of at-

tention, the consumer in an S/M scene: The sadist is only catering to his or her desires.

In theory S/M was a logical next step for the sexual revolution. The crisis in heterosexual relations in the seventies left many women thinking there was no way to reconstruct the sexual act as long as women remained powerless in the dominant culture. While feminism promoted mutuality and better communication, in practice men and women were still at odds in bed. S/M was one way to bring men and women back together again by offering them a form of self-conscious, carefully negotiated sex. Power could be rationed, doled out according to who wanted more—and who wanted less: "Submission" could be redefined as a crucial element in sex, and stripped of its automatic ties to the female gender. S/M gave equal license to both men and women to explore their weaknesses and their strengths.

In the formality and premeditation it required, S/M was almost a parody of the heterosexual interaction recommended by the liberated sex manuals of the seventies. The new, nonmedical sex advisers no longer assumed that the sexual act was bound to be mutually pleasurable. Some things would please one partner, while the other partner might need an entirely different set of stimuli. All they could hope to do was negotiate a fair enough exchange—a little of this for a little of that. S/M went beyond whispered negotiations to a more conscious recognition of the partners' different needs and of the impossibility of fulfilling them with perfect simultaneity. If heterosexuals in general were learning that good sex took work, practitioners of S/M had taken the further step of turning sex into a *project*.

But in other ways S/M was a repudiation of the sexual revolution. Not only was it overtly anti-egalitarian, but it ruled out spontaneity and any casual promiscuity. A woman would have to genuinely trust a man before allowing him to use handcuffs or leather straps; and a man, too, would be well advised to know something about a woman he wished to be dominated by. S/M was not for people who enjoyed making love spontaneously in the dark, or for people looking for a casual one-night stand. The process of gathering equipment, working out a fantasy, and then acting it out turns sex into an elaborate set of activities that most people simply don't have time for. Particularly for devotees rather than occasional explorers, S/M demands enormous attention and concentration—even an obsessive devotion to sex.

On the whole, the feminist movement is divided on the issue of S/M. Some see sexual variations, including S/M, as progressive openings within a culture that fails to support individuals who break the monogamous heterosexual standard. For Pat Califia, a self-described lesbian feminist sadomasochist and founder of an S/M society on the West Coast, S/M has an ideological function. It is a way of using sex to demonstrate real—in this case, female—sexual power: "S/M is not about pain," she argues, "but about power."[11]

Yet for many women who are practicing light S/M in its less ritualized, less extreme form, S/M is probably not so much an empowering force as it is simply a novelty, tantamount to experimenting with a new haircut. The process of buying the accessories and making preparations may be half—or much more than half—the fun. Not only the devotee but the curious novice has to invest in uniforms, equipment, instructions, and

more, very much like someone beginning a new sport.
At Patty's Place in Miami, a store similar to the Pleasure
Chest, the most popular items are ankle and wrist restraints. According to the owner, the clientele sees
nothing horrifying about the S/M equipment sold.
"S/M is something new to try," she told a *Time* reporter, "like redecorating your bedroom."[12]

S/M is in many ways a product of the modern sexual
marketplace, but elements of the ritual had been integrated into sexual practice long before Alex Comfort
put "Discipline" and "Chains" on the table of contents
page of *The Joy of Sex*. Sex for women has traditionally
involved a form of role playing considered so natural
that it was unconsciously integrated into the sexual act.
"Faking it," for example, is the most familiar element of
dramatic ritual in conventional, prerevolutionary sex—
which was itself a ritual in which men were required to
dominate and women to remain submissive. Strange as
ritualistic S/M may seem, power plays and role playing
are hardly unfamiliar terms of endearment.

For some women, S/M may have been an improve-
ment on the old, unconscious variety of sadomasochism
promoted by the marriage manuals of the fifties. At
least with S/M, a woman had a chance to be a consumer
in her own right, rather than being the passive instrument of male urges. She might even be able to dictate
the terms of her sexual encounters. And as with any
other new technique, S/M could be used to solidify the
bonds of a monogamous relationship, just as the more
daring could use it to make a conscious statement about
relationships of power. In either case, it provided an
expression for the fantasies of erotic domination and
violence that seem to figure so prominently in the

dreams (and nightmares) of both sexes, according to experts ranging from Masters and Johnson to Nancy Friday. For some women, S/M may simply have been a way of taking the guilt out of sex—as if, in the form of S/M, the sex itself had become punishment enough.

Still, S/M was a bizarre side trail for a sexual revolution that had begun in women's emerging drive for equality and independence. The pioneers of women's sexual revolution, whether or not they called themselves feminists, had insisted on a more self-determined, assertive form of female sexuality than the arbiters of "normal" heterosexuality allowed them. But the feminist aspirations that had originally inspired the sexual revolution had no control over its commercialized forms. In the sexual marketplace, ideals and causes have no place; novelty is all that counts—even when the novelty seems to subvert women's original impulse to sexual liberation. Of course, independent career women as well as unadventurous housewives could experiment with S/M without changing anything else about their lives or self-images. But S/M was still an admission that equality might not work—at least in sex —and that we might as well make the best of inequality, even in its most contrived and ritualized form.

S/M was not, however, the strangest denouement of the sexual revolution. In S/M, inequality is sexualized out of the context of everyday life and relationships. There is no relation between wanting to be a top in S/M dramas and being domineering and authoritarian in daily life, or between being a bottom and being a masochist in relation to a spouse or friends. By sequestering off sex into a realm of conscious ritual, S/M could still be consistent, in an odd way, with feminism or any other egalitarian belief system. But this is not true of the next setting into which we follow the sexual revolution: In the world of Christian fundamentalism, masochism is the prescribed role for women, and yet there, too, women's sexual revolution has been inexorably gaining ground.

5
Fundamentalist Sex
Hitting Below the Bible Belt

The women filling the auditorium were well-dressed, their hair meticulously arranged, their makeup carefully detailed. A hint of past, better times surrounded them, a whiff of the fifties in the tight control of their look. They were there to learn how to maintain that image: The theme of the seminar they were attending was "How to Be Beautiful Inside and Out." The workshop was part of a larger conference sponsored by the Christian Women's National Concerns, one group in the proliferating network of Christian right organizations. According to sociologist Joanne Young Nawn, an observer at the session, undergarments, those objects of beauty that are neither inside nor out, occupied a large part of the discussion. The need for a good bra was emphasized, since the sight of an erect nipple can apparently induce a man to uncontrolled lust. The audience was told that light, silky bras are too suggestive, especially during brisk cold weather, which makes the nipple stand out.[1]

To Nawn, the workshop was a "downright prurient" lesson in the embarrassingly detailed requirements for women who act as guardians of morality. Sitting on their pedestal of feminine modesty, they are expected to be totally womanly—sweet, passive, nurturing—yet at the same time they are held responsible for the lewd reactions of every passing male.

According to the sex experts of the religious new right, women must take responsibility for the way men treat them because men can't control themselves. The male is a victim of what one conservative Christian book calls the "Y chromosome factor," something in the male genes that makes "sexual arousal . . . much more quickly stimulated through eye contact." According to the authors, fundamentalist therapist George Rekers and his equally conservative colleague, minister Michael Braun, once they are stimulated, men cannot be expected to rein in their urges. Women must no longer tempt them by wearing, "even to public worship . . . clothing that would have been considered the attire cf a prostitute fifty years ago." Such dress creates a "problem" which can be solved if "Christian women will . . . accept the fact that they will be hopelessly out of style." But there is a silver lining for a woman who wears the proper attire. She has the privilege of providing "a feminine mystique that ennobles a man."[2]

Detailed fashion commentary may seem inappropriate coming from spiritual leaders, but the assumptions of the Christian right are theocratic: All aspects of one's life are theoretically subject to religious law. Yet, in the last decade, the sexual revolution has penetrated even the self-enclosed world of right-wing fundamentalism.

And the Christian right is fighting desperately to keep out—or to co-opt—the challenge.

Until very recently, Protestant fundamentalism occupied a peculiar backwater of American culture. Beaten back in the Scopes trial in 1927 (where, though Thomas Scopes was found guilty of teaching evolution, in spirit the agnostic rationalism of Clarence Darrow prevailed), fundamentalism retreated to rural and small-town America—especially the Southern Bible Belt. While mainstream Protestantism became increasingly secular in outlook—and spiritually undemanding—fundamentalists withdrew into a rigidly patriarchal and puritanical subculture of their own. But the sixties politicized fundamentalist leaders like the Rev. Jerry Falwell, who emerged in the seventies determined to enter the mainstream culture and combat the "Satanic forces" represented by feminism, the civil rights movement, gay liberation, and atheism. By the mid-seventies, fundamentalist leaders like Falwell and Pat Robertson of TV's evangelical "700 Club" had joined with more secular political right-wing leaders like Richard Viguerie, Howard Phillips, and others, to build a powerful network of fund-raising and lobbying organizations, political action committees, and publications. This network constitutes what is known as the Christian right, which ranges ideologically from Billy Graham on what might be called the liberal wing to—on the far, far right—paramilitary groups that urge white Christians to take up arms for the coming confrontation with Jews, nonwhites, and atheists. On this spectrum, Falwell and Robertson represent the mainstream of the Christian right.

While not all fundamentalists became political con-

servatives, any more than all conservatives became
true believers, the Christian right (which designates its
own enterprises and beliefs simply as "Christian") has
emerged as a major political and social force in America. Its leaders see nothing wrong with mixing religion
and politics. "The idea that religion and politics don't
mix was invented by the devil to keep Christians from
running their own country," Falwell has said.[3] It is this
ambition to run America as a "Christian republic" that
alarms less theocratically oriented Americans. But
there is no denying that the Christian right has struck a
responsive chord with a considerable segment of the
American public. By the mid-eighties, 40 percent of
adult Americans were calling themselves born-again
Christians, and another 20 percent counted themselves
as evangelical Protestants. Some twelve to twenty million people were tuning in to the huge Christian broad-
casting empire.[4]

The message put out by these media gospels,
whether overtly political or not, is deeply authoritarian,
and the ultimate source of authority is the Bible. Hard-
core fundamentalists stand their ground on the principles of biblical inerrancy: If it's in the Bible, it's the law,
no matter how times have changed in nearly two thousand years. Yet new ideas representing a unique interpretation of the Bible, if not a departure from it, have
found their way into the fundamentalist world. Feminism was far too radical for most fundamentalist
women, but the women's sexual revolution, which appeared without fanfare or formal organization and ex-
erted its influence first in the privacy of the bedroom,
infiltrated even this corner of conservative America.

Within fundamentalist ideology, it is automatically

assumed that women will marry. Like men, they are said to be governed by genetic programs, primarily those that create the need for marriage and maternity. "I was created to be the wife of Bailey Smith and the mother of his children," explains Sandy Elliff Smith, whose husband served two terms as president of the Southern Baptist Convention in the early eighties. (Smith is known for his comment that "God Almighty does not hear the prayers of a Jew.")

There is nothing wrong, however, with using a little innocent deception to advance God's marital designs. "There aren't many things more upsetting to the male ego than a female super-brain," advises one book for single Christian women. "If you're blessed with an unusual set of brains, use them, won't you, to keep from showing them too much?"

Once married, fundamentalist couples base their relationship on Ephesians 5:22–28:

> Wives, submit yourselves unto your own husbands, as unto the Lord. For the husband is the head of the wife, even as Christ is the head of the church; and he is the savior of the body. Therefore, as the church is subject unto Christ, so let the wives be to their own husbands in everything. Husbands, love your wives, even as Christ also loved the church, and gave himself for it.

This can be and has been interpreted in different ways by different people. A small group of women within the evangelical* movement see in the passage a message of

* Evangelicals, according to one view, generally "tolerate a somewhat broader range of Bible interpretation and cultural outlook," while for histo-

"mutual submission" between husband and wife, a sharing of power, a willingness to compromise. Fundamentalist interpretations emphasize the submission of the woman to her supposedly loving husband, but some hard-liners, by coupling Ephesians with a passage from I Timothy, infer that in principle all men have authority over all women:

> Let the woman learn in silence with all subjection. But I suffer not a woman to teach, nor to usurp authority over the man, but to be in silence. For Adam was first formed, then Eve. And Adam was not deceived, but the woman being deceived was in the transgression. (11:14)

Rekers and Braun interpret Timothy to mean that women are incapable of an active role in life by divine intention. According to them, Paul (the author of the letters to Timothy and the Ephesians) was going back to the creation story in order to draw

> upon principles of proper leadership that are expressed in human sexuality. . . . God does not act arbitrarily. God doesn't flip a cosmic coin in eternity and say, "Heads, I'll make man first." There was a plan to it. And when, under the pressure of satanic assault, that order of leadership was reversed and Eve initiated action, the result was catastrophic. . . . It is no wonder that Satan assaulted Eve first; she was woman, made by God to be ever so sensitive to

rian George Marsden, "a Fundamentalist is an Evangelical who is angry about something."[5]

spiritual input. She was made to respond, and Satan lured her to take independent initiative.[6]

THE "SECOND COMING"

One would think there was no hope for a sexual revolution given such doctrinaire, misogynist notions. But some fundamentalist women have proved themselves neither as docile as they are expected to be nor as ashamed of their "original sin" as their men might like them to be. They have learned to fight with the weapons on hand, receiving advice on guerrilla warfare from an unlikely source. In the early seventies, a born-again Christian housewife in Florida began to push the idea that if wives would act like homemaking Playboy Bunnies, they might gain a power advantage over their indifferent or domineering husbands. Her name was Marabel Morgan and her discovery of what women could do to transform their marriages won her millions of followers (and millions of dollars).

Morgan developed her principles of total womanhood after a typical argument with her husband, a wealthy lawyer named Charles. One evening he informed her that they were having dinner with business associates the following night. When Marabel pointed out that she had made other plans for the evening, Charlie said in "an icy voice, 'From now on, when I plan for us to go somewhere, I will tell you twenty minutes ahead of time. You'll have time to get ready and we'll do without all this arguing.' "[7]

Rather than throwing dinner in his face, Morgan submitted. Like the chastised child he considered her, she went to her room, but instead of sulking, she came up with a plan. "I'd tried to change Charlie, and that hadn't worked. Now I would have to change me." On the face of it, Morgan's newfound strategy was antithetical to feminism, yet it provided her with an area of initiative and control in an otherwise dependent life. While the scheme was centered on Charlie, and utilized the most traditional of society's expectations of what men wanted, there was little accommodation for Charlie in the actual plan; he was the object.

Morgan's program involved what theologian Martin Marty has called a "costume fetish [that] would dazzle Krafft-Ebing."[8] In her books *Total Woman* and *Total Joy,* she advocated that wives dress up as cowgirls and pirates (miniskirted versions), spies (with nothing on under the trench coat), elves, pixies, and strippers (with tea-bag tassles for those who couldn't afford costumes). Dressing as gorillas suited Morgan's piquant sense of sexual play as well. Men were not completely left out of the fun either. Morgan described one husband who came home as a scuba diver, changing in the men's room of the local gas station before arriving goggled and tanked at the door. Sex was to be inventive and unexpected. Wives were encouraged to have intercourse under the dining room table, on diving boards, trampolines, and bales of hay. Even the mundane bedroom was to be jazzed up with candles, edible massage lotions, and perfume-sprayed sheets.

All this was aimed at making the husband feel he was king of his home and master of a one-woman harem. "It is only when a wife surrenders her life to her husband, reveres and worships him, and is willing to serve him, that she becomes really beautiful to him . . . she becomes a priceless jewel, the glory of femininity, his queen!" Throughout the latter half of the seventies, millions bought this message through Morgan's books and Total Woman seminars. *Total Woman,* her first book, sold more than half a million copies in hardcover and had a first paperback print run of two million. The seminars, often sponsored by churches, cost about fifteen dollars, well within the range of the many lower-middle-class women who sought her help. Churches were quick to support Total Woman programs because, as Marty has pointed out, Morgan and her disciples were "massively evangelical," expecting "an imminent and literal Second Coming."

Morgan was born again, she says, after dropping out of Ohio State University and becoming a beautician. "There with the water running," she has written, "I was born again. I had asked Him to take me before, but I had never got any answers. This time I asked Him to take me and he took me. There was no bolt of lightning. Only peace. I was tickled to death."[9]

Despite Marty's tongue-in-cheek comments, many religious leaders took Morgan very seriously. The number of books sold were testimony to the need women felt to be "totaled," as the critics put it, by Morgan. Beyond that was the dawning recognition in the seventies that women and their sexuality could no longer be smothered under the sheets. Arguments on the merits of Morgan's ideas flew thick and fast in the popular and religious press, with the majority of commentators calling for an end to Total Womanhood.

Many religious observers were shocked by its message. "What hypocrisy," wrote liberal evangelical John Scanzoni of Morgan's advice that Total Women greet their husbands dressed only in an apron and black stockings, "telling a wife she is subject to her husband and then encouraging her to use sex to manipulate him." Jim Wallis, who represents the left wing of evangelical thought, complained that "evangelical wives and single women can now look like Hollywood starlets and feel good about it."[10] And journalist Joyce Maynard wrote, "The image of women presented in *Total Woman* is an ultimately demeaning one, and it demeans men as well; it represents women as weak and empty-headed complainers, obsessed with material possessions. I do not like to think what would happen to a Total Woman if her husband died." Probably no worse than would happen to her fundamentalist sister who had never paraded nude before her husband: all fundamentalist women are considered equally helpless, while Total Women at least have the benefit of "a book which simply reassures them," as Maynard wrote, "that sex is not sinful."[11]

Despite Scanzoni's misgivings, *Total Woman* was not primarily about manipulating men. It provided women with a frequently successful way to manipulate *themselves* out of an untenable situation. Morgan was overtly advocating submission, but she was decidedly subversive between the lines. In her books and interviews she displayed a spunkiness, an independent streak that belied her message. She publicly hinted that after working so hard to shake up a traditional marriage, it's a little difficult to go back to being suitably passive. "I rarely have to compromise," she once gloated, a surprising comment in any marriage. To Scanzoni and Wallis, Morgan may seem manipulative, but in a sense her idea that women should get something in return for their efforts, rather than merely submitting or sacrificing, is a decidedly feminist idea. If we are to service men and their homes, Morgan implicitly argued, why not get paid? Morgan received a new refrigerator-freezer soon after initiating her Total Woman techniques. Other rewards were flowers, perfume, lingerie, and jewelry. Soon enough, of course, she could afford these on her own.

But the biggest and best prize was a new sex life. In *Total Joy*, Morgan sounded as if she'd read either *The Sensuous Woman* or *Our Bodies, Ourselves*, both banned in most Christian bookstores. Women were encouraged to enjoy not only the playfulness and unselfconsciousness of sexuality, they were told to get pleasure for themselves. "Have him apply rhythmic pressure [to the clitoris] and don't give up,"[12] she advised. While her instruction wasn't very explicit, coming as she did out of a cultural milieu that had tried its hardest to ignore the social upheavals of the sixties, this was definitely revolutionary. Instead of a docile, possibly frigid wife for whom the vagina was the only thinkable sexual organ, Morgan held up the vision of a woman doing who knows what in her daily bubble bath.

In addition to a new sex life, Morgan tempted women who had been raised in the isolated fundamentalist tradition with a taste of the wider world. "I want to do something. I don't know what. Someday I wish I could travel," a Total Woman told Joyce Maynard while relaxing in her bubble bath with a glass of wine, preparing for her husband. "You have to understand, things were very different when I was dating. Today, all these kids living together and not married. . . . All these new things. Orgies and couples that switch off and girls having careers and living with their boyfriends. It's not for me. But you wonder about it." As the bubbles disappear in her bath, the woman murmurs, "I have my own checking account. It, you know, makes you feel more human. . . . Still, if I were doing it all over again, I wouldn't get married quite so soon."[13]

Morgan's message, whether salvation for unhappy housewives or merely a spark for a tired marriage, was a sharp break from traditional fundamentalism, which claimed, according to Christian commentator Lewis Smedes, "Sexuality is nature's strongest competitor for . . . loyalty to Christ. 'You cannot love God and sex.' " Given the choice (most fundamentalists assumed there was none), they'd have to give up sexual pleasure and concentrate on God instead. Morgan, operating out of the newly changed mores of the sixties and seventies, tried to turn the forbidden into something "as pure as cottage cheese," but with a little spice added. "Costumes provide variety without him ever leaving home," she wrote, promising men (and women) the same exotic thrill a secret affair might give.

Morgan's genius lay in eliminating the hang-ups that made sex inaccessible, while retaining the taboos that made it exciting. Traditional fundamentalist revivalism had drawn much of its dynamism from repressed sexuality. Anarchist Emma Goldman wrote of being nauseated by the "vulgar manner, . . . coarse suggestiveness, erotic flagellations and disgusting lasciviousness" of the early twentieth-century evangelist Billy Sunday. In Goldman's view, the "atmosphere of lewd mouthings and sexual contortions . . . goaded his audience to salacious hysteria."[14] For a sexual rebel herself, she seems to have had little sympathy for those who found their sexual expression where and how they could.

The steamy character of revival meetings has carried over to the present day, although less overtly "lewd" even by our more relaxed standards: The All-American pretty girls who sing their way through meetings, the beauty queens from Anita Bryant to Wonder Woman Lynda Carter who espouse fundamentalism, are an integral part of the television gospel scene and serve a purpose similar to the beautiful model selling cars in commercials. Morgan built on the subliminal erotic appeal of evangelism, moving the sexy girl into the home, giving the man a reason to come home at night and the woman a reason to welcome him.

Despite the criticism from some of her more liberal coreligionists, Morgan's impact on fundamentalist culture was profound. In the late seventies, books on sexuality suddenly began to appear on the shelves of Christian bookstores. These books were written by preachers and important fundamentalist leaders and usually coauthored with their wives—few men seemed willing to handle X-rated material alone. Many of the leaders no doubt recognized in Morgan's sometimes belligerent tones the same note of dissatisfaction they were hearing from the women in their own communities. There was an obvious market for Morgan's sexy, eccentric religion.

The response was a sudden proliferation of Christian sex books and manuals. As Jeffrey Hadden, coauthor of *Prime Time Preachers: The Rising Power of Televangelism,* put it, the new attitude seemed to be "if God gave you the plumbing, you might as well enjoy it." Some book titles, like *Tough and Tender, Celebration in the*

Bedroom, Intended for Pleasure, sounded as if they had been lifted from porn shops and blue-movie marquees, while others took a more homely and simple approach. In *Do Yourself a Favor: Love Your Wife*, Pastor H. Page Williams of Cairo, Georgia, offers the "talking cure" for sexual troubles:

> It is in talking with your wife that you let her take off your clothes, so to speak. She "talks off" your shirt of self-righteousness, your pants of self-sufficiency, your undershorts of self-pity. This is what stimulates her sexually.[15]

Some books contain surprisingly explicit examples from the Bible and real life on how to achieve a richer sex life. Reverend Tim LaHaye, for instance, advocated rereading the Song of Solomon for information on clitoral stimulation. LaHaye has long been a member of the national board of the Moral Majority, and in 1985, while working as a lobbyist for "traditional values" in Washington, he was described as "one of the shrillest of the Fundamentalist idealogues."[16] But LaHaye, writing with his wife, Beverly, was encouraging rather than shrill when it came to sex. The LaHayes provided specific positions: "the wife lying on her back with her knees bent and feet pulled up to her hips and her husband lying on her right side." This is the position described in the Song of Solomon, said the LaHayes, quoting verses 2:6 and, here, 8:3, "Let his left hand be under my head and his right hand embrace me." Following the interpretation of a Christian sexologist, they take this to be the best position for a man to "fondle" or "stimulate" a woman—i.e., masturbate her rather than rely on intercourse. They emphasized the centrality of

clitoral orgasms, described the physical changes a
woman goes through as she approaches orgasm, and
advocated mutual masturbation rather than intercourse on the first night together (the wedding night, of
course) because it "increases the possibility for both to
experience orgasm."[17]

"Everywhere we go to speak . . . the one question
we can count on is, 'What about oral sex?' " wrote religious therapists Clifford and Joyce Penner, the authors
of *The Gift of Sex*. And according to the LaHayes, they
were, at one time, receiving a question about oral sex
almost every week: "Husbands tend to desire this experience more than wives, but recently, because of the
many sex books on the market, there seems to be increasing curiosity on the part of women." The Penners,
fairly liberal, approved of oral sex. The LaHayes were
much more cautious. They pointed out that many people felt guilty about it, that venereal diseases, especially
herpes, could be spread this way, and "some girls find it
harder to reach orgasm in marriage by the conventional method after they have had the premarital experience of oral sex."[18] (It is not clear whether the marital
experience of oral sex has the same devious effect.) Ar-
kansas doctor and religious leader Ed Wheat and his
wife Gaye admitted in their book *Intended for Pleasure*
that the Bible doesn't forbid oral sex, but the practice
"definitely limits the amount of loving verbal communication that the husband and wife can have as they
make love."[19]

While most of their peers were ambivalent about oral
sex, the Reverend Charles and Martha Shedd, wed for
nearly forty years when they published their book, *Celebration in the Bedroom*, had moved beyond oral to

anal sex. The Shedds have been full of truly evangelical zeal over their newfound sex lives. They told a national audience on the Phil Donahue show that God had instructed them to "have more time . . . to celebrate in the bedroom," necessitating a move from their large congregation in Houston to a smaller, less time-consuming church. And later in the same show, they dismayed the LaHayes, also Donahue's guests, by admitting to a "whole drawerful" of vibrators, which were also "inspired" by God.

Whether explicitly or by suggestion, these books indicated (and continued to do so in the eighties) that submission, the cornerstone of fundamentalist thinking on women, was out when it came to sex. But only when it came to sex. Reciprocal pleasure was important, at least in this area of Christian life. Even here, sex was a commodity of sorts, just as it had become in the rest of American culture. Men were told if they wanted to keep a woman contented and in the home they would have to change their sexual practice. "Every wife has the right to be loved to orgasm," insisted the LaHayes, repeating Morgan's message that sex is the reward for being a good wife. Once men were "selfish lovers. . . . Sexual pleasure from the 'little woman' was assumed to be their divine right. . . . Such men were (and some still are) sexual illiterates." Today, said the LaHayes, the "modern" Christian man must educate himself to "tailor his affectionate passions to her emotional needs."[20] In what amounted to a virtual parody of seventies ideas about sexual give and take, the Charlie Morgans of the fundamentalist world were being asked not only to provide their wives with new couches and refrigerators but to take care of their physical needs as well.

Have orgasms and bubble baths and wine created a sexual revolution among fundamentalists? Is a newly discovered zeal for mutually satisfactory sex capable of transforming a way of life based on literal interpretations of the Bible, strict adherence to authority, and the submission of women? In many ways, today's pro-sex Christian leaders seem to have merely absorbed the messages of the women's sexual revolution into their authoritarian culture. Certainly there are some areas where fundamentalists don't even pretend to be interested in change. Premarital sex still amounts to spiritual destruction. In *Your Half of the Apple: God and the Single Girl,* Gini Andrews wrote that premarital sex

> tears living fibers apart . . . when you get up and put your clothes on and go home (or he does), you are not the same as you were. There's been a real mingling of life itself, and because God intended this to be a permanent, one-for-life arrangement, you are damaged when you try to treat it as something casual.[21]

To avoid the damage, Christian women were advised to pray with their dates before setting out for the latest movie or disco, and to avoid dark corners. At Jerry Falwell's Liberty University as recently as 1981, there was little point in praying before going out. Students were required to obtain written permission from the dean to go on dates, and only double dates were allowed. An interracial date had to be approved in writing by both sets of parents. Going out to a disco was grounds for suspension. To encourage students to obey these rules, uniformed guards with American-flag patches on their shoulders stood watch over a bridge that was the only exit from campus.[22]

When single men and women fail to live up to fundamentalism's regulations, the lapse appears to have greater consequences for women. According to the LaHayes, "Many a married woman suffers today from guilt and shame caused by indulging in [sexual intimacy] before meeting her husband. . . . We know of cases where couples had to leave their home churches after marriage because the wife couldn't face the man she was previously so intimate with before breaking the engagement."[23]

Men, apparently, suffer no such shame and can remain in their home church with impunity. Not surprisingly, many Christian women end up believing that being single is a punishment to be endured for as short a time as possible. "It's terrible to be single," says TV star Lynda Carter, who surely has had her choice of interesting men to date. "You're dating different people, and you don't know who to believe and who not to believe. You're constantly insecure without a mate or a real friend."[24]

FUNDAMENTALIST S/M

Despite the appearance of change, much remains the same in the fundamentalist world, proof that even the most feminist aspects of the women's sexual revolution can be co-opted by male authority. For the long term, the impact of a more modern, feminist—or feminoid— sexual ideology remains to be seen. New attitudes may be taking root that will someday be a powerful influence on the lives of fundamentalist women. For the short term, the changes are mainly superficial. Fundamentalist women have hardly moved forward, despite Marabel Morgan and the proliferation of sex books. Little can touch the bonds that hold most of these women in place because the prerequisites for independence—education, careers, worldly experience—are not there. The traditional fundamentalist family tends to treat women as servants, moral misfits, or virgin goddesses—anything but equals. For many couples, sex is still something done by a man to his partner in the dark. While Marabel Morgan is pushing Saran Wrap party clothes for at-home wear, many women are still changing into their nighties in the bathroom and crawling into bed in the dark, to do whatever an inexpert and insensitive husband demands.

Not that sex is *always* a perfunctory duty. Repression, as the Victorian era showed, can offer up its own rich lode of sexual imagery, which relies on being unacknowledged and illicit for titillation. As Morgan proved, roles play an important and acceptable part in fundamentalist sexuality. In role playing, it is not just important to have—and be put in—one's place, but all participants must know exactly what that place is. Fundamentalists like to define exactly what men and women are, using the old standbys about men being "aggressive, dominant, logical, independent, active, ambitious, and task-oriented," while women are "submissive, intuitive, dependent, nurturant, supportive, patient, and person-oriented."[25]

Such concrete definitions can force a woman to flee into the more flexible world of the imagination. For fundamentalists, the sultry femme fatale can also be the

Lilith side of Eve, who was created to be the good girl, "God's helpmate for man," as Dr. Wheat says. While the dogma may call for a quiet unassuming woman, the Biblical message of her evil heritage is part of woman's sexual secret; a reason to be despised, objectified, and desired—particularly in a darkened bedroom. In real life the seductress has too much autonomy to be a fundamentalist woman.

Another fantasy, more accessible to the light of day, emphasizes the submission and helplessness of women. During the seventies one Christian sex expert even endorsed teaching women how to act out the exciting game of "little girl." Helen Andelin, founder of Fascinating Womanhood, which was almost as popular among Christian women as the Total Woman program, recommended that her followers, when settling an argument with their husbands, "stomp your foot. . . . Or, beat your fists on your husband's chest, pouting: 'You hairy beast. . . . How can a great big man like you pick on a poor little helpless girl? I'll tell your mother on you.'" For fashion pointers, Andelin sent her "domestic goddesses" to the little girls' department of their local stores to see what the prepubescent crowd was wearing. While Total Women were shopping for sexy negligees, Fascinating Women were searching—not all that successfully, if you were a full-figured gal—for what would be kinky stuff in any other context: Mary Janes and anklets, gingham and ruffled dresses.[26] Morgan at least restricted her fetishes to the sexual act. Andelin's consumed a woman's life; she dared not step out of character and ruin the image by appearing intelligent, competent, or the least bit independent. Fascinating Womanhood was a life sentence.

Women's helplessness, their submission to their role if not their man, could be dangerous. Despite the promise that the submission of the wife will be matched by the kindness of the husband, fundamentalist imagery sometimes vies with that classic of sadomasochism, *The Story of O.* Bev LaHaye has called on wives to adopt the attitude of Jesus Christ: "The willingness to be humbled, to be obedient unto death, and to be submissive." LaHaye's instructions to the "spirit-filled" wife could match the rules O was presented with upon entering the chateau where she was to be held in bondage by its male caretakers. Compare these two quotes.

LaHaye:	O:
As the woman humbles herself (dies to self) and submits to her husband (serves him), she begins to find herself within that relationship. A servant is one who gets excited about making somebody else successful. . . . You can live fully by dying to yourself and submitting to your husband.[27]	You are here to serve your masters . . . you will drop whatever you are doing and ready yourself for what is really your one and only duty: to lend yourself . . . you are totally dedicated to something outside yourself.[28]

The tone might just be silly if it weren't for the seriousness fundamentalists have attached to wifely submission. If the line between normal and perverse sex is as thin as experts in the fifties thought, fundamentalist women are walking on a razor's edge: They are expected to submit and ultimately *enjoy* their degradation. The idea of pleasure never occurs to O, old-fashioned masochist that she is, but Bev LaHaye promises *excitement* in the service of a total master. Yet she offers no recourse for the times when a master's whims take a malicious turn. Andelin's naughty little girl getting spanked, Bev LaHaye's "excited" servant are both symbols of women's brutalization in right-wing Christian culture. There are few alternatives for the woman who doesn't conform. Rekers and Braun claim there are times when a wife can refuse to submit to her husband, as in "the sad story of a Christian wife whose non-Christian husband encouraged her to extend her sexual favors to a business associate in order to help the husband close a big deal."[29] That example leaves quite a bit of room for abusing the principle of wifely submission. Even the books dedicated to helping men treat their wives better assume that women need to be dominated. "When you bully your wife and push her around and overpower her with cursing and anger, you are really sick. You have a sick marriage," warned Pastor H. Page Williams. But he was not surprised some men fell into this pattern. "The reason this is such a big temptation is because a woman wants to be ruled. Her great desire is to be subject to her husband, because God has ordained it so . . . that's the curse of a woman . . . her desire to be ruled leaves her wide open to be abused." His solution? A call for absolute, but enlightened monarchy—the man must be a "good king" in his castle.[30]

Some fundamentalist ministers show no sympathy for women, despite what they may see and hear in their offices. "Wife-beating is on the rise because men are no longer leaders in their homes," one minister told an interviewer. "I tell the women they must go back home and be more submissive. I know this works, because the women don't come back." University of Texas sociologist Anson Shupe described one woman he interviewed whose second husband had been beating her for four years. When she finally got up the courage to see her minister about the problem, he told her the abuse was her "payment" for divorcing her first husband.[31]

Except for a small group of evangelical feminists, there is surprisingly little outcry from within fundamentalism against the principle of absolute male rule. According to evangelical feminist Virginia Mollenkott, Jesus was a feminist, calling on the early Christians to treat each other, man and woman alike, with greater kindness than their culture had previously shown. "Jesus was calling for mutual submission" in the context of that era, she says. But she and others like her are fighting an uphill battle in the face of many women's conviction that submission is something they can live with and adapt to. In *Who Will Save the Children*, a documentary film by Vicki Costello, Mary Morris, young and fresh-faced, sits with her minister and her husband, describing not only why she is opposed to the Equal Rights Amendment but why, thanks to the new direction fundamentalism has taken, she no longer needs the ERA: "You don't have to be a doormat anymore. That's not what submission means. It means we're equal but we each have certain things we do better than the other. Like diapers. I change diapers better than he does."

Even women committed to the idea of submission have their way out when they need one. Women who could never dream of making a Total Woman's demands on their man can still get through the long day of washing clothes, making beds, cleaning up after everyone—and through an equally long night of joyless sexual relations—by pushing God's presence in their lives to the ultimate, but perhaps obvious, end point. They dream of a love affair with Christ.

Gini Andrews, for example, calls on single women to dedicate their lives to Christ and not some male's sex drive: "Which is freedom: being the love-slave of the Lord Jesus Christ who went through physical, mental, and spiritual anguish beyond your wildest imaginings to buy you back from Satan's camp, or being slave to a human being's sex drives—yours and/or his?"[32] Other women turn to God for relief from an unhappy marriage. "I prefer to snuggle up under Jesus' love in bed," one woman told sociologist Nawn. Or they may resort to the more encompassing fantasy of yet another woman who imagined her husband fading from her life. "A lovely young wife," as Ed Wheat described her, she said that it was

> often difficult dressing to go out for the evening with her husband because she knew in advance that he would not treat her the way she longed to be treated. So she developed the habit of thinking of the Lord Jesus as her friend and escort for the evening. "It helped me tremendously," she said. "I looked my best for Him, I behaved myself for Him, and I was constantly aware of His steadying presence with me!"[33]

A Boston area wife told radio producer Aimee Sands, "I like a man who knows he's a man. Somebody that can be tender when it's necessary. Somebody that can tell you to cut it out when you're being foolish. There are not many men around today. Jesus Christ is real to me. No other man satisfies."[34] Fundamentalism has given some women a place for their passions, by letting them turn on to someone who can't push them around the way a mere mortal can.

This is not just a fantasy that women conjure up in private, nor are they expected to feel embarrassed about it. Ministers themselves often set the stage for the dream, referring to sexual intimacy that "could never be complete without the three persons—man, woman and God." The Wheats, offering yet another interpretation of the Song of Solomon, explain a mysterious voice in the bedroom King Solomon shares with his lover as "God Himself . . . the only One [who] could be with the couple at this most intimate time." Andrews advised single women to get in the habit of going on dates with God or even taking him shopping: "Ask Him to help you find the right dress, or the new car, or even the gloves you had in mind. You may be surprised at what good taste He has and find you've spent far less money than you'd feared."[35]

As an outlet for unexpressed frustrations, this fantasy of a love affair with Jesus is both a part of religious doctrine and beyond it. Nawn, in her analysis of the Christian right, has pointed out that fundamentalism has "put God the man back into religion." God is depicted as a physical participant in fundamentalist life, not an ethereal, divine presence. Compared to the actual men who run the lives of the women on the Christian right, God is a psychological amulet, a more loving consciousness than that provided by many conservative fundamentalist husbands.

Jesus may make it possible to survive one's marriage to a good king, bad king, or a violent one, but the underlying theme of the relationship is still sadomasochism. The spokesmen of the Christian right don't call it that, for pointing out its correspondence to a known sexual "variation"—in itself a highly secular notion—would open up the prospect of alternative sexual and social themes. But the ritualized partnership, the role playing, the overwhelming concern with power and authority, match the sadomasochistic game—with a critical difference. This is no game; it doesn't end when the sexual encounter is over; there are no rules allowing the woman to end the scene. Better orgasms and more sensitive partners can't make a difference because they are bought at too high a price: accepting a slave mentality not just for a finite sexual encounter but for an entire life.

Ironically, while feminist ideas about sex have been moving into fundamentalist culture, fundamentalist ideas about monogamy have been moving into the mainstream. Fundamentalists may be trying to work new sexual techniques into patriarchal marriages, but sex outside of marriage remains the work of the devil. Most religious conservatives regard extramarital sex as a kind of mark of Cain branding women's psyches with the "searing knowledge that something unique was lost along the way."[36] But we can also see in the ranting against this extramarital experience the fear that male authority might be undermined. When Bev LaHaye comments that men can distinguish between sex and emotional commitment but women cannot, she is really saying women *must not* make this distinction. When women are not dependent on one man to fulfill

their needs, men have lost control over them. The fear
of women's sexual independence has become a major
theme of the eighties, one that indicates not only the
growing strength of the Christian right, but the powerful, lingering influence of sexism in American culture.

6
The Politics of Promiscuity
The Rise of the Sexual Counterrevolution

Ellen, at thirty-four, has made what she considers a "nice little life" for herself. She works for the local telephone company and has managed to buy a small house on the outskirts of Santa Fe. She has what used to be called All-American good looks—straight, gleaming hair, and clear blue eyes. She is single, has had numerous boyfriends, and is currently seeing one man, whom she has been dating for the last two years. By her own description she is a "cowgirl," with a rough and ready attitude toward sex. Her present relationship is just one more phase in her continuing sexual exploration. The late sixties, when she made her first discoveries of her sexuality, were, she says, "one of the most intense periods of my life. I had learned nothing about sex at home and was constantly randy as a teenager. It was a relief to let my needs explode. I had a chance to discover what I liked sexually, who I liked. I made a lot of demands on men too; I chose them for their sexiness or sensuality. Amazing discovery that I could do that."

Ellen's enthusiasm is typical of the generation of women who came of age sexually at a time when repression was coming undone. Their newfound sexual freedom brought the added benefit of a healthy confidence in their bodies—and in their ability to live, at least part of the time, without being seriously involved with a man. Even if they were heterosexuals, other women might still offer the warmth and emotional intimacy that was previously expected of a sexual relationship. They could also, if they chose, experiment with bisexuality or eliminate men from their lives altogether. Such women were realistic: Casual sex was neither heaven nor hell, but it was an important part of their sexual experience.

Nevertheless, by the early eighties a backlash was brewing against what was pejoratively called female "promiscuity." The media began to metamorphize the modern woman, who had been practicing her sexual negotiating skills throughout the seventies, into an old-fashioned girl looking for moonlight, flowers, and commitment. Women who didn't fit this new stereotype were portrayed as hopelessly misdirected. Instead of thinking only about sex, suggested Mike Morgenstern in his 1984 book *How to Make Love to a Woman*, they ought to be considering a "return to traditional sex roles and the warmth these can bring." Despite the enthusiasm women brought to the sexual revolution, this new revisionism inevitably began to feed on their doubts, undermining the positive feelings of many who had enjoyed the freedom of casual sex.

Given the extent of the changes women's sexual revolution had brought to heterosexuality in one brief generation, it is not surprising that some people were confused. As one woman plaintively told a reporter for *New York* magazine in 1984:

> When I was growing up, my mother told me it was important to be a good wife and mother. I was sent off to college to find a man. And then Gloria Steinem said, "No, you want more than marriage, more than motherhood." So I rejected my parents' values. . . . I threw myself into my career. I looked totally androgynous. Is it any wonder my relationships got all screwed up?[1]

This woman was expressing the dilemma of anyone caught in the midst of a revolution—political or cultural. The old verities disappear; choices have to be made where none were demanded before. Freedom may be exhilarating, or it may just bring on a bad case of anxiety—or both. Men probably felt more insecure than women, since their position of strength was being called into question. One male respondent theorized in *The Hite Report on Male Sexuality:*

> The "sexual" revolution, then, is a threat to [men] because it reduces their dominance. If a woman happens to "offer herself" . . . to a man more often because of the "revolution," he's even more threatened than before because the offering is not dominance.[2]

Under the circumstances, a backlash may have been inevitable. But this backlash was ignoring, and in some cases actively denying, the very real statistics and testimony that pointed to women's increasing enjoyment of sexual independence. Ellen was typical of the millions of women who were exploring sex and eager to talk about it. "Sex is an important part of my life," she says. "I'm not willing to do without it if there's no permanent man in my life. I take for granted the pleasure I get. Of course, it's not always easy to find a man to provide that. But I've picked guys up everywhere. I'm more cautious now, but I once spent several months with a guy who was sitting at the table next to me in a restaurant. It was really just sex, but we had a good time for a while."

According to surveys in several major magazines, by the late seventies a majority of women of all ages had accepted with pleasure progressive attitudes toward sex. *Redbook*'s editors were amazed, and awash in responses, after they published their questionnaire on sex in 1975. Almost 100,000 women, overwhelmingly white, married, and middle-class, wrote in and their comments left the surprised editors exclaiming, "Women are becoming increasingly active sexually and are less likely to accept an unsatisfactory sex life as part of the price to be paid for marriage." The study also found that a "considerable number" of *Redbook*'s readers were having affairs while happily married to men they loved, and nine out of ten of the young women who responded were engaging in intercourse before they married.[3]

As statistics, these women were remarkably on target with a survey five years later of *Cosmopolitan* readers, who were supposedly a much more sexually aggressive crowd. "*Cosmo* girls," too, had rushed in, eager to discuss their varied and active sex lives. Helen Gurley Brown described her fears that the survey would never be answered, since it required that "the reader not only . . . answer seventy-nine questions, scissor the pages out, put them in an envelope and address it, but add her *own* postage." Yet soon after the questionnaire ran in the magazine's January 1980 issue, Brown had herself photographed "sitting on a stack of questionnaires that reached nine-feet high. After eight weeks, when we finally stopped counting, more than 106,000 *Cosmo* readers had filled in and mailed their sex-survey questionnaires to us . . . this was the biggest response to *any* magazine survey in history and surely the largest sex survey ever conducted." Many of *Cosmo*'s readers were as sexually satisfied as *Redbook*'s (they reported that, on average, they had had nine lovers) and a little more brazen to boot, in keeping with their favorite magazine's image: "I have lovers because sex feels good," said one, and another claimed, "I have lovers because what else is there in life that's so much fun as turning on a new man, interesting him, conquering him?"[4]

Another round of surveys in 1983 by *Playboy, Family Circle* and *Ladies' Home Journal* concentrated on wives, depicting them as "sexually enthusiastic, confident, romantic and satisfied." One criterion: the number of married women having extramarital affairs. From Kinsey's broad estimate that 6 to 26 percent of married women were having affairs, the statistics jumped in the early 1980s to anywhere from 21 all the way to 43 percent, depending on the magazine conducting the study. Among *Playboy*'s readers, young married wives were "fooling around" more than their husbands.[5]

Some women were downright raunchy in surveys where, thanks to anonymity, they could tell all: "At this point, unless he's well hung, I just wouldn't be interested in him. I know this must sound a little obscene, but it's important to be honest about what you need," said a twenty-nine-year-old stockbroker in *Savvy*'s 1985 "Sex and Success" poll of female executives. A real estate broker said: "I've bedded down with some of the men to whom I was showing apartments. . . . I'd say to them, 'This is the kitchen, this is the living room, and here's the bedroom. Want to try it out?' "[6] At the other end of the spectrum, a more soberly presented 1985 survey by the Roper organization found that eight out of ten women thought single women should have the same sexual freedoms men did—up from six out of ten in 1970.

Women's sexual revolution had a great many committed converts, but men were lagging behind. In the Roper poll 43 percent of the men surveyed wanted a traditional marriage, "in which the husband was the sole provider and the wife ran the house."[7] The traditional man seemed to have equally conservative sexual views. Many surveys still showed a large majority of men who did not think women should engage in premarital sex or have extramarital affairs. As one female veteran of the New York singles scene said, "It's the same old 1950s rules of the game. . . . I've found a lot of fear of my own sexuality. Beneath the rhetoric lie the same old attitudes."

THE DEATH OF SEX?

At the end of 1982, *Esquire* ran a cover story titled "The End of Sex."[8] The article was illustrated with a photograph of a funeral wreath of dying roses laid over a tombstone which read, "The Sexual Revolution, R.I.P." Sex, as we have just seen, was far from dead. But a certain notion of sex—loving, nurturing, long-term sex —was gone, wrote George Leonard. He announced "the trivialization of the erotic climaxes in the practice of 'recreational sex' in which sexual intercourse becomes a mere sport, divorced not only from love and creation, but also from empathy, compassion, morality, responsibility, and sometimes even common politeness."

Was Leonard bemoaning the death of sex after all, or the birth—already over a decade old—of female sexual autonomy? He implied that women were making it too easy: "Recreational sex palls not so much from its immorality as from its dullness. The plot can be summed up, Hollywood style, in three sentences: Boy meets girl. Boy gets girl. They part." Many of the women reading that article had experienced enough of heterosexuality, whether pre– or post–sexual revolution, to know that recreational sex had always been part of the traditional male repertoire. Whether in 1950 or 1980, casual sex had always been *the* macho symbol, and very few men were complaining as long as they controlled the action.

Men like Leonard were responding to the little-discussed fact that the true heart of the sexual revolution was a change in women's behavior, not men's. "There hasn't been a change in male sexual patterns in the twentieth century," historian Vern Bullough told *Time* in 1984. As that article pointed out, "Studies tend to agree that changes in male premarital sexual behavior since the '30s have been rather modest. Premarital sex rates for women more than doubled between the 1930s and 1971, and sharply rose again to a new peak in 1976."[9]

In the early seventies many young men had taken to the sexual revolution with seeming delight; a whole new pool of sexual partners was now available. Their pattern of sexual activity hadn't changed, but the object of men's casual attractions was now more likely to be the girl next door than some woman of "dubious" reputation. In the fifties, sleeping with a "nice girl" was like walking through a china shop: "You break it, you buy it" held true in both cases, and "shotgun" marriages were common. But by the late seventies, marriage was no longer an obvious conclusion to sexual relations. For one thing, a man could not assume that the woman he was sleeping with was monogamously involved with him. The new premises seemed so difficult for some men to accept that they stumbled all over their ambivalent feelings when they talked about sex. "I know it's a contradiction, thinking it would be nice to marry a woman who is a virgin, yet I want a woman who knows how to enjoy a good time in bed. This doesn't mean I want a woman who has been promiscuous. I'm flattered when a woman comes on to me, but I wonder if she's not just a little too forward," a computer programmer told sex educator Carol Cassell, the author of the 1984 book *Swept Away: Why Women Fear Their Own Sexuality.*[10]

Where women had once participated wholeheartedly, some were now having second thoughts when confronted with male ambivalence—and sexism. Despite all the talk of the sensitive, feminist "new man," too many women claimed to be meeting men who simply could not let them participate with equal control in a sexual relationship. "You have no idea what it's like out there," a woman bus driver in Philadelphia says. Married and divorced, she's been happy to "date around and sleep around." But, she says, "Sometimes they treat me like just another woman who 'puts out' for them. Or they think *I* want commitment and to some men that justifies treating a woman like dirt." It seemed that the kind of man who insists on lighting a lady's cigarette or opening the door for her wasn't ready for a woman who would open the door to new sexual experiences. As British author Wendy Holloway points out, men had more to lose when women used sex, rather than emotional ties, as a criterion for a relationship. "Men can represent themselves according to a set of assumptions in which they are not in need of . . . anything that would make them vulnerable." But, she adds, the invulnerable man often relies on a woman to provide the emotional warmth that eludes him. Women who insist that sex need not involve a love affair are thwarting men's ability to decide when they want access to intimacy.[11]

The relationship between sex and intimacy was confusing for both sexes. Substantial numbers of women, such as this respondent to the *Cosmo* survey, still felt guilty about sex:

> There are nights I say goodbye to a lover to whom I've just given the greatest ecstasies in bed, and I think to myself, Here I am in my

dangerous Greenwich Village apartment, with
its fire escapes and dingy staircases. Maybe
someone will break in and rape me during the
night. Or kill me. Will this guy I'm saying
goodbye to ever wonder about me in the
morning?

For other women, economic insecurity was still a strong
incentive to see sex as the gateway to marriage. As
another *Cosmo* reader said:

In the past a man used to have to offer a relationship in order to get sex. Tat for tit. But
now, since so many women give sex so freely,
the men offer nothing—and we women must
accept this, even if we don't like it. Throughout the centuries women have gotten the
short end of the stick. We're still getting it.[12]

There was more at stake here than just a misunder-
standing between the sexes. Women's sexual liberation
had touched social bedrock, threatening ideas about
gender, dependence, family, and marriage. Some people didn't like to be touched there.

The increasing ambivalence of both men and women
coincided with the rightward political drift of the eighties. Under Ronald Reagan the United States Congress
voted funds for "chastity centers," a concept more acceptable to conservatives than family planning or sex
education. The new conservatism brought back the
idea that women were responsible for sexual activity
and therefore to blame when a pregnancy ensued. In
this climate attacks on abortion became both rhetori-
cally and physically violent. Between 1982 and 1985

there were over a hundred bombings and other violent attacks on abortion clinics around the country. With the threats to abortion rights and the growing dangers from sex-related diseases, the message to women was that the risks associated with sex—casual or committed— were escalating unacceptably.

The conservative political atmosphere reinforced the anxieties of men and women who were struggling to assimilate the sexual revolution, and the media were quick to pick up on the new mood of hesitation and nostalgia. By the mid-eighties, the nearly unanimous message presented by the mainstream media was that women were fed up with casual sex. There were few criticisms of men; this was a campaign against women and their sex lives.

THE MEDIA FIGHTS CASUAL SEX

A successful TV executive is quoted in a 1984 article in *New York* magazine on being single in the city: "Maybe I'm a victim of arrested development," says the woman, thirty-two, "but I don't feel old enough to be married. Right now I just want to concentrate on my career and enjoy my life."[13] Her comments, typical of many working women, are followed by those of a psychotherapist specializing in adolescent psychology:

Two earmarks of adolescence are the beliefs that time is limitless and choices are unnecessary. Many singles in their thirties have adopted that same attitude. In the past, there were certain developmental tasks, like marriage and child-rearing, that signaled one's adulthood. But in today's urban culture, it's acceptable to postpone those tasks as long as possible.

Patricia Morrisroe, the writer of this article, never questions the strange idea that a woman who maintains a career and supports herself is not mature. In the same article a thirty-six-year-old financial analyst in search of a wife says that "somebody over thirty is a definite negative." He would also "prefer a virgin. 'Why not?' " he asks. But there are no therapists in evidence to comment on *his* immaturity.

The article, which is really on the terrors of being single, is illustrated with bleak drawings of the unmarried life. One shows a woman snuggling up to her pillow in an otherwise empty bed. In another, a business-suited woman in glasses grabs for but misses a tossed bridal bouquet. The piece, titled "Forever Single," ends with the message that singles had better learn to compromise in their search for companionship.

In the same vein, when "NBC Reports" ran the documentary "Second Thoughts on Being Single," early in 1984, it implied that women's primary goals are love and security: They need to get married, while men try to avoid marriage. The program began with the statement that women of the "baby-boom generation" are "fed up with modern American men, and modern morality." They want to get married, they want a family, and, said one of the program's experts, sociologist Pepper Schwartz, they won't get those things if they're sexually active, because "men [don't] like them to be very sexually experienced." In case some women might resent men's dictating the range of their sexual experience, Schwartz also insisted that women really weren't meant for casual sex:

> I don't know many women and I haven't studied many women who think of sex as something they could do and never see the identity of the man they had it with. . . . [There are] many men who, as soon as they've had their sex, would like to say "goodbye, that was great; we both enjoyed it, and I don't want to know you." That is a thought that is pretty foreign to most women.[14]

The program showed attractive, educated women with good jobs who seemed hopelessly lost at singles gatherings; others were working out every day—not for pleasure but for vanity, in the hope of simulating the body of a teenager. Then there were women mooning over other people's babies, proof positive to the viewer that they needed a man and a family. A long parade of academic experts was called upon to show that women were naturally monogamous, or if they weren't, had better be. Tired clichés emanated from experts like Dr. Nancy Moore Clatworthy of Ohio State University, who said, "The farmer used to say that a man certainly wouldn't buy the cow if he could milk the cow through the fence."

Boys and girls have always had very different play patterns, said a psychiatrist, implying that it was therefore no surprise if their sexual proclivities also differed dramatically: "Little boys tend to play organized games like baseball . . . little girls tend to play . . . in pairs." And if some would argue that those differences were mainly due to socialization, Dr. Donald Symons of the University of California at Santa Barbara was called in to present his belief that sexual behavior is biologically determined. Man's prehistoric role, Symons told narrator Jack Reynolds, was "to impregnate as many healthy looking females as possible." Women, on the other hand, had nothing to gain from "random copulation" and faced "enormous risks by becoming pregnant." Evolution, he said, had made them congenitally monogamous.

These experts all assumed that women hated casual sex, but they offered no explanation for why so many women were engaged in it. In fact, several women on the program explained that the problem wasn't the sex, it was the attitudes of the men they were sleeping with. "I've lost lots of guys because I didn't go to bed with them," explains one single. But, says another, "If you go ahead and give in to your desires . . . and you do go to bed with him, then lots of times you really will lose the man because they, without even realizing it, feel like you've been too quick and too easy, and if you're that way with them, God knows how many other people you're like that [with]." The only solution, according to one woman, was to become a "born-again prude." If there were women who were still willing to fight with men over their right to sexual freedom, NBC never found them.

More surprising than *New York*'s profile of a group of neurotic singles or NBC's born-again prudes was the new tone of *Cosmopolitan,* the bedside companion of many practicing singles. Once symbolized by the tough, sultry woman on the back page of national newspapers who might have been saying, "I can't tell Tom,

Dick or Harry apart. Who cares? I guess you could call me that *Cosmo* girl," the magazine now ran stories such as "Why We Don't Like No-Strings Sex" and "Go Slow: Make Love the Old-Fashioned Way." One article, titled "Sketches from the Single Life: Intimate Glimpses of Five Unmarried Women," read like a fundamentalist tract on the wages of sin. Sex and the single girl? The *Cosmo* girl was going to have to pay a price.

> Anne awakes with a start. She's thrown off the covers and is shivering slightly. The landlord cuts the heat at midnight, and without glancing at the clock, she knows it's later than two. That's when the old lady on the fifth floor starts howling. She's into ghostly moans now— aargh, aargh . . . Home . . . where roaches waltz insolently over the dish drainer . . . and where breakfast is a baloney sandwich and dinner a bowl of cornflakes.[15]

What has brought on this misery? As far as we can tell, it seems to be penance for the days

> when she was by herself so much that she'd sometimes take a man home just for the company. (Morning light on the unlovely skin of a stranger; her body pulling away from his, as if from a disease.)

Anne has just one man she sleeps with now, but things aren't much better. Paul, her lover, wants to spend only weekends together, grouses at her, and is wary of commitment. The vignette about Anne ends on a forlorn note. She will give up this hopeless love affair and buy a puppy for companionship, temporarily alone again in her building where "the old lady's moaning is soon to commence." The consequences of the single life seem to be loneliness and near-insanity.

The other four women's lives aren't any better. One is unemployed, longing for her one true love, who refused to stand by her when she lost her job: "Girls these days operate at a terrible disadvantage. Nancy's pretty and charming and can cook and knows she needs to have a career. But that's not nearly enough to get a really good guy." Another, Nina, "opens sludgy eyes to a steamy July day . . . it gives her a headache!" As far as her current romance with a live-in lover, the best she can say is [I've] "known worse relationships, that's for sure." Most of the time she'd just as soon not have sex with him, for there's no "surging passion." Through Nina, the article presents a textbook example of the wages of guilt. Coming from *Cosmopolitan,* these morality tales were surprising. Some of the magazine's more sexually sophisticated readers, who had once counted on it to reinforce their lifestyles, must have felt as though they had stumbled onto an issue of *Reader's Digest*—circa 1950.

SEX RADICALS SEARCHING FOR LOVE

Another serious blow to mainstream acceptance of casual sex came when two women, famous as sexual mavericks themselves—if only in their writing—executed their own about-faces. Erica Jong, who had delighted many female readers with her breezy, picaresque approach to sex in *Fear of Flying,* was, ten years later, not so sure that women had benefited from the sexual revolution. Her 1984 book, *Parachutes and Kisses*, brought Isadora Wing, her alter ego and heroine of *Fear of Flying*, up to date sexually, and while it documented the frequency and variety of Isadora's sexual encounters, the pleasure of the hunt had definitely given way to the search for true love. Passion was no longer an end in itself. Jong began her book with Isadora's musings on the sexual balance sheet a decade after the revolution: "The world has certainly changed. For one thing there is more oral sex. For another, more impotence. For a third, sex is ubiquitous and yet also somehow devoid of its full charge of mystery."[16]

One could argue that Isadora Wing's cynicism arises from her poor choice in lovers. In *Fear of Flying* the assortment of husbands and lovers included a psychotic who tried to kill her; a conductor "who never bathed, had stringy hair, and was a complete failure at wiping his ass"; a psychiatrist who refused to kiss or speak to her when making love ("each orgasm seemed to be made of ice"); and Adrian Goodlove, mostly impotent, dirty and given to farting in public. No wonder she was now looking for romance.

Wing is, after all, a fictional character. Yet Erica Jong had clearly given some thought to the drawbacks of the sexual revolution. "Many women discovered," she commented in an article surveying the influence of the birth control pill, "that the freedom to say yes to everyone and anyone was really another form of slavery. Repeated, meaningless, one-night stands without commitment did not satisfy their hunger for love and connection, and so the so-called sexual revolution was really more a media myth than a reality." The author who had once celebrated the joys to be found when women chose and experimented with lovers now called sexual liberation a "pseudo event."[17]

Another equally influential woman was on the same trail. Germaine Greer, one of the more glamorous exponents of early feminism, had been the perfect media spokeswoman for some very radical sexual ideas. But after years of espousing sexual freedom, Greer reverted to a philosophy suspiciously like that of the fundamentalist right. In 1984, during an interview following the publication of her new book, *Sex and Destiny*, she told a reporter that by exchanging "fidelity" for "promiscuity," women had traded one form of restriction for another: "The sexual revolution never happened. Permissiveness happened and that's no better than repressiveness."[18] But in *The Female Eunuch* she had asked women, as a "revolutionary measure," to refuse "to commit themselves with pledges of utter monogamy and doglike devotion." She had called for the destruction of "the polarity of masculine-feminine." To achieve this, "individual women [must] agree to be outcasts, eccentrics, perverts, and whatever the powers-that-be choose to call them."[19]

Now, in *Sex and Destiny*, she changed her mind. She recounted with obvious embarrassment how, in the early sixties, she had foisted her feminism on the people of Rossano Calabro, a small Italian village where she had gone to write her doctoral dissertation. She flouted local rules on women's behavior by traveling into town on her bike alone, refusing to lower her eyes when she spoke to men, and wearing a bikini to the beach. Rather than admitting that she might have moderated her stance to accommodate an alien culture, Greer now seemed to regret the spirit of independence that had inspired her actions.

She claimed to have realized her mistake while still working in Rossano Calabro. One day she had an "awakening," in which she suddenly noticed the sexuality of her one friend in the village, sixteen-year-old Rosetta. "Sex was in the air that Rosetta breathed: she was ripe and the ripeness was all. . . . Rosetta . . . had more confidence in her female sexual power than I would ever have." Rosetta, the product of a local "morality . . . much sterner than anything the fat priest preached in the marquis's rose-pink chapel," had never even spoken to the young man she was pledged to marry (although Greer had caught her secretly eyeing his crotch). Yet her sexuality left Greer so envious that she was transformed, she says, knocked, like Saul on the road to Tarsus, right off her seat. "I gave my bicycle away to a little boy, and I took another little boy as my chaperone whenever I went out. I lengthened my skirts and kept my eyes down if a man came towards me, and I wore an old bathrobe to the beach."[20]

But Greer was not simply another woman lost to some fantasy of femininity (as though she could re-create Rosetta's blossoming adolescent sexual awareness through copying the forms of female repression). She had, after all, written *The Female Eunuch* several years after her revelation in Rossano Calabro about women's proper role. In that book all her feminist anger had been presented with clarity and wit. Yet a decade later she was glorifying women's sexual repression.

Soon after the publication of *Sex and Destiny*, Greer told a reporter that she regretted waiting to have a child: "Like many women, I chose not to have a child when I could have. Then when I thought I could fit one into my life I found out I couldn't conceive." Critic Linda Gordon believes this is at the heart of Greer's revisionism. A book "about fertility . . . written by a woman suffering from infertility . . . elicited my sympathy," wrote Gordon in *The Nation*.[21] But, she continued, Greer is "generalizing on the basis of what seems to be her personal response"—and forgetting, one might add, that millions of women, including herself, have fought for the idea that their sexuality is not linked absolutely and eternally to their reproductive capacity.

IT HITS THE SPOT

While women were trying to sort out the mixed messages they were receiving from the media about their sexuality, the medical profession once again entered the public dialogue on sex. Science, in the form of the pill and Masters and Johnson, had helped validate the sexual revolution. Now the same authority was used to debunk the pleasures of variety. Psychologists who had once taken up the cause of sexual freedom and experimentation now adopted a more cautionary stance. Despite some popular exceptions like Dr. Ruth Westheimer, known as Grandma Freud to her legions of fans, liberal ideology was being swamped by the tide of experts welcoming a return to "traditionalism . . . the fad of the future," as one commentator termed the new sexual conservatism. Media therapists, offering advice on radio and TV shows or in newspaper columns that reached millions of Americans, had a strong influence on this trend. Dr. Toni Grant, once described as the most "glamorous" practitioner of public therapy, responded to what she viewed as a mismatch between female and male sexual attitudes by claiming women wanted only love and marriage:

> Uninformed people have misled us to believe we could separate sex from feelings, but very few of us are able to. The sexual act is a more profound event for women, based on the nature of femininity itself. We want long-term bonding and union with a man.[22]

Pepper Schwartz, the NBC singles expert and co-author with Philip Blumstein of *American Couples,* a book described as "the largest and most comprehensive study of American couples ever undertaken," believes with Dr. Grant that women have their priorities wrong. "A lot of women went out and wanted to be adventurous," she said:

> Over time, they found a number of things . . . they weren't getting married. I think they found that they weren't getting respect and they weren't getting love, and over time, it gets real old to have a long sexual dating experience with someone and then [have them] leave you for someone else.[23]

The idea that love and sex were inseparable for women was not a new one, but it was being presented as if it were scientific revelation. The pressure on women to become monogamous was increasing steadily. All that was needed, it seemed, was a way to restore to the sexual act earlier, simpler pleasures. It had become too varied, too difficult to define and pin down. Science would try to resolve this sexual dilemma.

> I have always had orgasms, but I never had much stimulation when the penis was completely inside my vagina. In fact, sometimes my excitement and arousal would end abruptly when the penis entered me completely. I have always been most excitable when the penis was only one-half or one-third its way into my vagina. Now I know exactly why—at that point it hit my "magic spot."

Most readers might assume this woman is referring to her clitoris. Until the early eighties, she probably would have been: The clitoris was our rediscovered magic spot, although the penis might not have been the best instrument to stimulate it. But now, clitoral sexuality's association with female sexual assertiveness seemed to inspire some sexologists to head back into their labs. Their new "scientific" goal was to relocate the penis, which had been missing in action, and bring it back where it belonged—into the vagina, of course.

To slow down the sexual revolution it was necessary to explode the notion that sexual practice should be wildly experimental. The clitoris was too free an agent; to bridle the female libido, and return the lead to men, intercourse had to be brought back into the act as the main event. A debate long since put to bed—clitoral vs. vaginal orgasm—was reawakened. Although feminist writers such as Anne Koedt and mainstream researchers Masters and Johnson had shown in the sixties that all orgasms originated in the clitoris and depended on clitoral stimulation, whether direct or indirect, the new experts insisted on producing new distinctions between orgasms. It made good copy and, more important, was an attempt to reestablish the role of the medical profession in defining sex.

The story of the G spot began in 1950 when Dr. Ernst Grafenberg, a German gynecologist, published an article in the *International Journal of Sexology*. He pinpointed a previously ignored erotic zone located "on the anterior wall of the vagina along the course of the urethra." His findings languished in obscurity for years. Then, in the late seventies, Alice Ladas, Beverly Whipple, and John Perry, a psychologist, nurse, and minister/sexologist respectively, came upon Grafenberg's research and decided to conduct interviews to see if his claims could be validated. Their subsequent book, *The G Spot,* did not give the impression there was much science to their method.[24] There were no charts or statistics to support conclusions. Instead, the authors of *The G Spot* insisted that a surprising 100 percent of 400 female volunteers, all of whom were examined by a nurse or a doctor, were able to locate their G spot. The book was filled with testimonials from these and other women who insisted that only vaginal orgasms would do.

Ladas, Perry, and Whipple said that the vaginal area of the G spot, when properly stimulated, swells and produces an orgasm that is distinct from—and better than—a clitoral one. They also claimed, without getting too specific, that many women ejaculated a fluid through the urethra during a G-spot orgasm. Their statistics: When they asked "coed audiences" if they had experienced female ejaculation, about 40 percent raised their hands. The authors said the G spot was a "vestigial homologue of the prostate"—hence the fluid.

Just as peculiar as the sudden discovery of an unsuspected bodily fluid were the acrobatics necessary to achieve the new orgasm. *The G Spot* advocates jettisoning the missionary position, which would have automatically classified the "new" orgasm as old. Instead they insisted that "man is designed as a quadruped and therefore the normal position would be intercourse *"a posteriori."* This enabled men the maximum thrust, because, as one of their male interviewees said, "Certain women really want you to pound them."

Women were turned on their faces, in a position suspiciously similar to one used for anal sex. Indeed it seemed that one of the authors' goals in pushing the G-spot theory was to bring the anus into focus, for, they implied, anal sex was what men really wanted to perform on women and to have performed on themselves. Men were capable, the authors said, of the same multiple orgasms as women, if their prostates were given enough strokes. The best way to stimulate the male prostate, said Ladas et al, was to insert a finger into the anus. If there were women too squeamish to give their men multiple orgasms in this fashion, the authors issued a warning: "One of the reasons some men may enjoy homosexual relationships is that they often provide more frequent stimulation of the prostate than heterosexual involvements."

The G Spot also presented the insidious notion that women's clitoral obsessions were driving men to homosexuality. But the male tendency to flee from sexually demanding women could be combatted. According to the promoters of the G spot, foreplay was not a good idea, since any stimulation of the clitoris merely distracted women from locating their vaginal centers of pleasure. Men could simply return to immediate penetration without having to worry about women's orgasms. The newly discovered mass of tissue in the vagina would supposedly take care of that. Without the worry, men would not have to resort to homosexuality for old-fashioned, self-centered sex.

From *The G Spot* it was easy to infer that women who had still not discovered their sunken treasures were suffering from some sort of vaginal amnesia. But thanks to John Perry's electronic perineometer, which could be ordered through the mail, women could perform exercises in their homes to strengthen the muscles that held the penis in place. Help was on the way, as long as women were willing to move backward into the eighties.

But the attempt by *The G Spot* authors to reinstitute traditional sexual intercourse seemed merely crude when compared to the very real fears about Acquired Immune Deficiency Syndrome, which began to appear in the early eighties. Once it became clear that AIDS was not restricted to gay men but could be spread during heterosexual intercourse, the hysteria surrounding the disease was an epidemic in itself.

Sexually transmitted diseases such as syphilis, gonorrhea, and herpes, as well as AIDS, lend themselves to public moralizing. But in this case, the backlash against sexual promiscuity was well established before AIDS became a topic of general concern. When it did, it was all too easy to use the tragic new disease to reinforce the developing sexual conservatism. The early response to AIDS centered around the concept of "safe sex": the use of condoms or spermicidal jellies, a reduction in the number of sexual partners, and elimination of drugs such as amylnitrate that can affect the immune system. But as public health educator Nick Freudenberg noted in 1985, the recommendation of safe sex quickly degenerated to no sex. The director of the National Centers for Disease Control, Dr. James Mason, announced that to control AIDS it was necessary to control sex. One California health official suggested that anyone who fell within the risk group or had had sex with someone in the risk group since 1978 should not exchange body fluids with anyone else. "This proscription," said Freudenberg, "rules out most known forms of sexual activity (including kissing) with another person for hundreds of thousands, possibly millions of people." The real motivation behind the "no sex" message, he continued, was "political and religious, not scientific. It seeks to impose on all of us the notion that sex is moral only within marriage." Once again, "objective" scientific thought was being used to further moral proscriptions.[25]

While most people did not yet advocate extremist "solutions" to AIDS, such as quarantines and ID cards for possible carriers, many began to reevaluate the role of casual sex in their lives. "The day of the one-night stand is over," a tennis instructor told a reporter for the New York *Times* in 1986. "I go to bars now to drink, not pick up women, and if I go out with a woman I don't sleep with her until I check up on her history and her reputation." Women too are displaying a new caution. "The fear [of AIDS] gets in your head and it can have a chilling effect on your libido," a California woman reported in the same article.[26]

Casual sex, of the one-night stand variety was definitely on the wane, but celibacy was not the alternative. Many women admitted to approaching new sexual relationships with some trepidation, yet the complete absence of sexuality in their lives seemed unthinkable. Caution and a new kind of intimacy have taken on greater importance as the public waits to see how and if AIDS will spread beyond the initial high-risk groups. For safety's sake women who engage in casual sex are spending more time getting to know their partner's sexual background and as an added precaution using condoms. For everyone seeking either a permanent partner or a temporary relationship, there are of course no guarantees. Someone who unknowingly slept with a carrier in 1980 might pass on the disease in 1986, even if they were monogamous for most of the intervening years. "It's strictly a roll of the dice," said one single woman. Living with that knowledge hasn't been easy, but many women have made adjustments which they hope will limit their risk and which have improved their sex lives in other ways as well. They say they prefer, for reasons of safety as much as health, to know a man more than one night if they are going to let him into their home and bed, or go to his. They also prefer sharing responsibility for birth control and safety techniques with a man as opposed to having sole responsibility in this area. Thus, after improving the odds to the best of their ability, most men and women are still willing to play the game.

CAN THIS REVOLUTION BE SAVED?

In the midst of reaction, the women's sexual revolution was being reappraised as part of an attempt to make sense of the events of the past two decades. Since the analysis the conservatives were offering was inherently antiwoman, the question of who controlled the direction of the revolution became one of the most critical issues to be debated. But feminism, which had helped initiate the sexual revolution in the first place, was now deeply divided over it. Some women, described as "cultural feminists," advocated an ideology that, in emphasizing women's "natural" traits, ended up glorifying attributes painfully similar to the reactionary clichés the conservatives were pushing. To these feminists, women's sexuality could be described in terms of gentleness, nurturance, and "circularity," as opposed to aggressive penetration. Others—who should perhaps be called the new radical feminists—argued that the women's sexual revolution had to be open to all possibilities or a new tyranny would be created. Any attempt at this stage to define women's sexuality was premature and too limiting.

Australian-born feminist Lynne Segal suggested that we still had a long way to go in the sexual revolution before most women would experience a real change in their lives. "Many of the ideologies surrounding 'sex' have remained *unchanged* over the last hundred years," said Segal. "Whatever the questioning which is going on, and whatever the tolerance for 'deviance,' sexuality is still seen in terms of its reproductive functioning, symbolised by a genital heterosexuality which men initiate and control." By restating the important

but easily obscured point that sex with men will always
be based on the nature of men's and women's relations
—collectively and individually—Segal offered a reminder that love, romance, and marriage could be just
as painful in a sexist society as anything a sexual adven-
turer might experience.[27]

If women could acknowledge that the problem was
greater than the particular man they slept with, they
could also insist on their right to continue pushing forward the frontiers of female sexuality. Lesbian activist
Amber Hollibaugh seemed to be speaking for more
than just the gay women she was describing when she
called for a new kind of "speak-out," in which women
would admit their secret yearnings.

> Who are all the women who don't come gently
> and don't want to; don't know yet what they
> like but intend to find out; are the lovers of
> butch or femme women; who like fucking
> with men; practice consensual S/M; feel more
> like faggots than dykes; love dildoes, penetra-
> tion, costumes; like to sweat, talk dirty, see
> expressions of need sweep across their lovers'
> faces; are confused and need to experiment
> with their own tentative ideas of passion; think
> gay male porn is hot; are into power?[28]

The media were not telling the story of the women
who spoke up and questioned sexual orthodoxy, nor
was it looking for the women who had become, essentially, the avant-garde of sexuality. They were women
like Diane, who, with her short, bright red hair, flashy
clothes, and uproarious laugh, is a mixture of punkette
and flash:

I have what I call the "gang boyfriend motif." I
have one boyfriend I've had for eleven years
[she's thirty-eight]. He's been married twice in
that time, and I know and his wife knows we're
both better off not having him full-time. He's
my main man. Then I have other boyfriends,
usually out of town, who I see fairly regularly. I
also have one other boyfriend in town, who I
really like a lot. They all add up to one big
boyfriend, and all my needs get taken care of.
It keeps me out of the bars—that's what I call
the "desperado motif."

Her main man once asked her to marry him, but "I
knew we couldn't live together. We can love each other
and I know we always will. It's more fun this way."

Diane's gang boyfriend is proof that a better man—
Mr. Right?—does exist, only it takes ten men to make
one. Obviously this is not an option for most women;
they literally don't have the time to juggle ten men into
their schedules, even if they would like to. Yet Diane
represents a small but important cadre of independent
women who *are* promoting sexual solutions. These are
the women who laughingly call themselves "sport-fuck-
ers"; who, given the choice between promiscuity and
repressiveness, as Greer saw it, will choose promiscuity,
although they would prefer not to be faced with such
absolute choices. These are women like this:

I love the mystery of something new . . . the
physical and emotional possibilities of testing
myself and him. The variety *is* the turn-on. All
those sex manuals insist that it takes experience with a partner to have good sex.

It is not necessary that these women speak for all of us. But their solutions are more than symbols; their choices are not so extreme that they have no relevance. Those on the frontier of sexual choice keep alive options that might otherwise be buried under a reactionary avalanche. What seems experimental and marginal at one time may become an important option for all women at another time. Shulamith Firestone, for example, was once regarded as a radical feminist whose ideas were provocative (she recommended separating reproduction from sexuality by having all babies born outside the womb) but had little application in the "real world." Yet in 1970, in *The Dialectic of Sex*, her ground-breaking study of the need for feminist revolution, she wrote:

> The most important characteristic to be maintained in any revolution is *flexibility*. I . . . propose . . . a program of multiple options to exist simultaneously . . . some transitional, others far in the future. An individual may choose one "life style" for one decade and prefer another at another period.[29]

As Firestone thought, casual sex should be a choice, not a duty imposed by ideology and not a privilege to be whisked away as soon as the political climate turned conservative. But sometimes even options are not negotiable; women have come too far to surrender the range of possibilities opened up by their sexual revolution.

Conclusion

Victories that we do not claim are never really ours to celebrate or improve on; and women's sexual revolution remains, for the most part, unclaimed. True, the benefits of this revolution are ambiguous: The sexual double standard is still firmly rooted in the minds of men, or at least enough of them to make the practice of heterosexuality a risky, potentially bruising enterprise for women. The benefits are unevenly distributed: Women who are young, economically independent, attractive, are much more likely to have come out as victors than the majority who are "old," "unattractive," overworked, and constrained by family and financial necessity. And the benefits, the achievements, can be rolled back at any time by new threats to women's sexual health and self-determination: Abortion could be made illegal, just as it has already been made financially inaccessible to women in poverty. New sexually transmitted diseases, such as AIDS, which may have the potential to spread to the mainstream heterosexual society, could send us in full retreat to involuntary chastity or monogamy.

But to imagine that there was only "the" sexual

revolution and that it was a victory for men and a joke on women, to see women as victims even of their self-chosen ventures, is not only to falsify the past but to foreclose the future. A victory, no matter how partial and unfinished, is worth little until it has been acknowledged. Otherwise, when it comes to the next leap—in our own lives or in the next generational upsurge of women—there will be no ground, no freshly conquered territory, to stand on. And in the case of women's sexual revolution, we accomplished more than we sometimes allow ourselves to see—certainly more than a mass culture grown jaded with "revolutions" and stylishly cynical about "liberation" is willing to *let* us see.

First, we challenged the old definition of sex as a physical act. Sex, or "normal sex," as defined by the medical experts and accepted by mainstream middle-class culture, was a two-act drama of foreplay and intercourse which culminated in male orgasm and at least a display of female appreciation. We rejected this version of sex as narrow, male-centered, unsatisfying. In its single-mindedness and phallocentrism, this form of sex does imitate rape; it cannot help but remind us of the dangers and ambiguities of heterosexuality. At best, it reminds us simply of work: "sex," as narrowly and traditionally defined, is obsessive, repetitive, and symbolically (if not actually) tied to the work of reproduction.

We insisted on a broader, more playful notion of sex, more compatible with women's broader erotic possibilities, more respectful of women's needs. Our success in redefining sex can be measured not only in the reported proliferation of "variations" (not all of which are women's innovations, of course) or surveys documenting changes in sexual routine and practice, but in expectations: Twenty years ago the woman dissatisfied with sex was made to believe she was lacking something; the woman who selfishly advanced her own pleasure was made to worry about being less than normal. Today, it is the woman whose marriage still confines her to phallo-centered sex who knows she is missing something; and it is the woman who does not know how to negotiate or find her own way to pleasure who wonders if she is different, abnormal.

It is strange that such a major change in what we think about ourselves and expect from others should be so little heralded today. Perhaps we let our sexual revolution be trivialized by a media eager to absorb each novelty and, in the process, make it instantly passé. Sex would not be the first arena of women's initiative to be trivialized as the price of minimal acceptance: Demands for a more equal division of labor in the home were initially dismissed as frivolous—and only grudgingly accepted as just—and the same is true of feminist efforts to make everyday language include both sexes. Or perhaps we sometimes minimalize the sexual revolution because we have forgotten already how bound we were to the old version of sex, how limiting it was, and how unimaginable the alternatives seemed.

In addition to redefining the physical act of sex, women's sexual revolution challenged the old "meaning" of sex as it had been interpreted, most recently, by medicine and psychiatry. By focusing on what can be directly perceived and experienced—sensations, the anatomy of sexual response—we did, as the critics so loudly complained, take some of the "mystery" and "magic" out of sex. This was perhaps coldhearted and unromantic of us, but we had come to understand that the "mystery" was simply a form of obfuscation. The grand and magical meanings—eternal love, romance, and, always, "surrender"—were there in part to distract us from the paucity of pleasure. Draped in mystery and mythic themes, sex itself was an act of sublimation for women: not an immediate pleasure to be appropriated but a symbolic act to be undertaken for ulterior aims—motherhood, emotional and financial security, or simply vanity.

Early feminist writers on sex, Barbara Seaman and Shere Hite among others, insisted, at least implicitly, that sex should have no ultimate meaning other than pleasure, and no great mystery except how to achieve it. They realized that for *women* to insist on pleasure was to assert power, and hence to give an altogether new meaning to sex—as an affirmation of female will and an assertion of female power. The old meaning, which in one form or another was always submission to male power, could be inverted.

These are no small achievements—the re-making and the reinterpreting of sex—and it would be both excessive and inaccurate to claim that women did it all or did it all for the cause of sexual liberation. Women made the changes, but many factors contributed to the possibility of change. Improvements in birth control in the sixties, especially the pill, gave women a sense of freedom and flexibility that the more cumbersome, "on-site" methods had never done. The effect of the pill may have been as much psychological as practical; even those who became disillusioned as a result of the side effects and risks gained the conviction that contraception *could* be safe and unobtrusive, and could, if the technology only existed, be the burden of men as well as women. Legal abortion was also, as its opponents correctly perceive, a powerful factor in women's sexual liberation. The more decisively sex can be uncoupled from reproduction, through abortion and contraception, the more chance women have to approach it light-heartedly and as equal claimants of pleasure.

Gay liberation was another contributing factor, no matter how remote it may have seemed from the lives of many who benefited from women's sexual revolution. Gay men and lesbians held out a vision of sex utterly freed from the old reproductive "work ethic" that haunts heterosexuality: Sex could be sheer play; it could be the celebration of a temporary affinity, or the indulgence of long-standing lovers. Lesbianism in particular defied the old medical notion of sex centered on heterosexual intercourse as the psychic and physiological means to fulfillment. If lesbian love could be impulsive, passionate, and satisfying—even if only among some "other" women one had read or heard of—then heterosexual sex was merely an option, and thus subject to a new standard of comparison. One could ask, in imagination, how interesting and enthusiastic a partner one's lover or husband would be if he were constrained from bringing the male organ into play. One could imagine, even more subversively, what sex might be like without a trace of the heterosexual drama of male power and female subordination.

Perhaps most of all, women's sexual revolution was made possible by women's growing economic independence from men. Independence is not the same as affluence: Women still earn just over sixty cents for each dollar earned by men, and women college graduates still earn less, on the average, than male high school dropouts. But independence, even in straitened and penurious forms, still offers more sexual freedom than affluence gained through marriage and dependence on one man. The young office worker who earns barely enough to rent her own apartment, the married woman who brings in her own share of the family income, even the single mother on welfare, have more sexual options than a "kept" woman, married or not. In fact, one reason for the stigmatization of welfare, and hostility to it, is undoubtedly that it offers women independence from individual men and, hence, a certain measure of potential sexual freedom. Male fears of women's sexual independence are at least partly responsible for the cruelly inadequate level of support available.

The last change, especially, has been a long time in the making. Traditional patriarchy rested on the economic interdependence of each member of the family, usually in an agricultural setting. Survival depended on participation in the common effort and in the hereditary division of labor—men plowing, women weaving and hoeing, and so forth. For a woman outside of the family economic unit there was only danger, destitution, rape. With the rise of the market system and a *social* division of labor—still plotted, of course, along gender lines—women's economic independence became at least a possibility. In a sense, women's sexual revolution began with the first "working girl" who kept part of her wage to buy a ribbon or hat, or who was able to afford a room of her own with a door that could be shut. In the 1960s and 1970s, a majority of women entered the work force and gained, if not exactly "liberation," at least the financial leverage to imagine being sexual actors in their own right.

Yet, having come this far in our sexual revolution—much further than our mothers and certainly our grandmothers could have imagined—we seem to find cause less for celebration than for ambivalence and anxiety. For what we have achieved, the remaking and reinterpretation of sex, is something that women both deeply want and deeply fear.

So powerful is the backlash today, and the official new mood of sexual conservatism, that we have to remind ourselves of how ancient and deep that desire is. It is expressed not only in the risks taken by a few exceptional women who defied sexual norms in the name of their own freedom—Emma Goldman, Victoria Woodhull, and Frances Wright are among the better-known examples—but by the repressed history of women's most incoherent, apolitical upsurges. Mass female adulation of the male androgynous rock star who represents sex freed from ulterior motive and daily necessity predates Beatlemania by many centuries. In the Dionysian cult of ancient Greece, women abandoned their household responsibilities for nights of frenzied dancing and worship of the beautiful young god. The witches of fifteenth- and sixteenth-century Europe were accused of similar excesses centered on Satan (who may have represented a god surviving from pre-Christian religion), and perhaps they did indulge in orgiastic rituals, though we have only the witch-hunters' word for it. Certainly their sexuality was at issue, as well as their daring to *assemble,* by night, in what were believed to be wanton rites.

But for most women in traditional societies, the possibility of noninstrumental sex, sex without the price of lifelong subordination to one man, was something glimpsed only at rare events—village holidays, religious festivals, carnivals. The carnival foreshadowed some of the best features of modern urban life: a public space apart from the hierarchy of the family, and crowds large enough to offer temporary anonymity and the license that went with it. In our time we re-create the carnival—or at least a diminished, modern version of it —in the discotheque, singles bar, or in the colorful, impersonal spectacle of consumer culture. We are drawn, as women have been for ages, to the possibility of celebrating our sexuality without the exclusive intensity of romantic love, without the inevitable disappointment of male-centered sex, and without the punitive consequences.

At the same time, though, women have grounds to fear sexual liberation, even their own. The fear is not irrational or neurotic, for if sex is disconnected from marriage, childbearing and family commitments, women stand to lose their traditional claims on male support. The teasing, instrumental sexuality prescribed for single women before the sexual revolution had a purpose, after all: to "land" a man, and to claim him as one's breadwinner for life. If sex is "free," then so, potentially, are men; and women are left to fend for themselves in an economy that still drastically undervalues women's labor. This was a dilemma that the radical feminists of the late sixties and early seventies, who boldly proclaimed the link between sexual liberation and women's liberation, did not always seem to grasp—

or, if they did, to sympathize with. Perhaps they imagined change coming suddenly and conclusively in all areas at once, so that no woman would have to fear financial ruin—or emotional desolation—if both women and men were free to express their sexuality.

But women *are* more vulnerable than men to the hurts and dislocations of a society that is sexually more free than it is just or caring. Women still bear the risks and costs associated with contraception and abortion. If they become mothers they undertake a disproportionate responsibility for their children—in most cases, *all* the responsibility if their marriage dissolves or if they have not married in the first place. If they do not become mothers early enough they may spend their prime years worrying about whether they ever will; men's lives are not constrained by the same biological deadline. If they are unmarried and on their own for any reason, they will, in most cases, have a hard time supporting themselves in an economy that still views men as the only legitimate breadwinners. And, sadly, women still "depreciate" sexually far faster than men: The gray hairs and wrinkles that lend character to a man's appearance only sabotage a woman's. One result is that divorced men are much more likely to remarry than are their ex-wives, and the gap widens ominously with age.

It was the fear of liberation that helped motivate the antifeminist backlash that began in the 1970s. Women who oppose abortion often cite its potential to free *men* from the obligations of marriage and parenthood. The fear is that if abortion is a woman's choice, then there will be no way to convince men that children are, in part, their responsibility too. Furthermore, sexual freedom for some women—any heterosexual women—seems to threaten the marriages and financial security of others. In a similar vein, women who opposed the ERA cited women's vulnerability, especially financial vulnerability, if the "protected status" of wives were undermined by egalitarian legislation. (Not that marriage, and the slender possibility of alimony after it, ever offered reliable, long-term protection from poverty. The male breadwinner could always leave, or simply spend his earnings on his own pleasures.) Better then, from an antifeminist perspective, to resist change and seek to retie the knots linking sex, marriage, and the economic dependence of women on their husbands.

The fears are real; so, too, is the desire for a freer, sexually happier life. Nor do the fears and the desire divide neatly into demographically distinct groups of women. It is not only young, attractive, self-supporting women who champion sexual freedom; just as it is not only middle-aged, financially dependent married women who worry that the same "freedom" could mean poverty and loneliness for them. In fact, very often, it is the same woman who feels both the fear and the desire. We *are* ambivalent; we seem almost to be stuck.

If there is a way out of the ambivalence, or at least a way to resolve it into alternatives and choices, it has to be a *feminist* way. We do not say this in a spirit of dogmatism but on the basis of our own experience. Feminism is not a "line" or a rigid set of beliefs. Rather, it is our only collective way of making sense of things *as women*. As radical feminist Kathy Sarachild wrote over a decade ago, feminism is a way of asking, "What's good

for *women?*" Feminists will differ on the answer; some
or all will be wrong at least some of the time. But the
feminist milieu of discussion, analysis, and respect for
individual experience is still the only space we have in
which to ask that question.

For the most part, feminism has tended to stand back
from the sexual revolution it helped to initiate. This is
not only because mainstream feminism has shied away
from controversies peripheral to its more central goals
of economic and political rights for women. Nor is it
only because feminists are, rightly, less concerned with
the beneficiaries of social change than its victims, the
women exploited by men's most callous versions of sexual liberation. There is another reason. In the last decade and a half, many feminists had arrived at their
own judgment not only of the sexual revolution but of
heterosexuality itself, and that judgment—without
ever being announced or formally debated—has
tended to be profoundly negative.

We are talking not about a superficial and unexam-
ined kind of puritanism but about a deeper kind of
insight: Feminists came to understand that sex and gender are not so easily separated after all. That is, sex as an
act or activity is not so easily disentangled from gender
as a social arrangement in which women, from as far
back as there is history to tell us, are unequal and inferior. As the Australian socialist-feminist Lynne Segal
writes, sex is, above all, "the endorsement of gender."
Heterosexual sex, and especially intercourse, is a condensed drama of male domination and female submission. The man "mounts" and penetrates; the woman
spreads her legs and "submits"; and these postures

seem to ratify, again and again, the ancient authority of men over women.

To put it another way: Heterosexual sex has had many uses, but it has had, over and over, one social meaning, and that is male domination over women. Midcentury psychoanalysts reinforced this meaning with theories of innate female masochism, and their views filtered into a body of sex "expertise" that prescribed sex as a ritual of husbandly domination and wifely submission. Ordinary men reinforce the same meaning every day when they tell their adversaries to "get fucked." This is not just an accidental limitation of the language: Sex, or women's role in it, is understood as a humiliation no man would want to endure.

So no wonder feminists have retreated from the subject of sex as well as the project of sexual liberation. In the late nineteenth century, feminists accepted the social meaning of sex as female subordination and saw it as an ordeal that women would endure only for the sake of motherhood. Contemporary feminists who campaign against pornography do not go so far as to say that sex itself is an ordeal or insult to women, but what else can be meant by their frequent insistence that every *representation* of heterosexual sex—however "soft-core"—is an insult to women and an assault on our rights? For if sex is the ratification of male power, then will it not always be a secret refutation of everything feminism stands for? Does feminism have any real option but to be puritanical or, what almost amounts to the same thing, utterly silent on the subject of sex?

But silence is itself defeat. Just as you cannot have sexual liberation without social equality for women, you cannot have equality in every other domain and an

unacknowledged ritual of male domination in the bedroom. You cannot have feminist rationality in the light
of public discussion and archaic dramas of power and
violence in the dark. Sex cannot be left as a lingering
biological embarrassment, something we try to put behind us as we campaign for our public rights. Feminism
has no choice, then, but to confront sex—to challenge
its social meanings—or be undone by it.

In fact, thanks to women's sexual revolution, there
has never been a more auspicious moment for feminism to grapple with sex as an opportunity and an issue.
We did challenge the narrow, heterosexual definition of
sex as the touchstone and standard for sexual experience. And we did call into question the social meaning
of sex. Without the ancient consequences of pregnancy
and dependence on male support, sex could "mean"
anything we wanted, and could just as well symbolize
our own widening aspirations as women.

Quite apart from our conscious efforts to re-make and
reinterpret sex, sex changed and diversified in ways
that implicitly mock the old and presumedly natural
meanings. Where, for example, is the great drama of
domination and submission when a woman buys masturbation aids from a mail-order catalog? What happens
to the meaning of that drama when two women—butch
and femme lesbians—can play all the parts? More profoundly, perhaps, S/M—by making domination and
submission into a consciously chosen and deliberately
scripted ritual—deprives these venerable themes of
their "natural" role in heterosexuality. This is not because ritualistic S/M is widely practiced (we have no
real idea of how prevalent it is), but because it is now
widely *known* as a potential option or variation. As an

imaginable option, it provides an ironic commentary on what has traditionally been understood as normal heterosexuality. If roles can be assumed as easily as costumes, and even traded off for variety, then male power is not the majestic theme our bodies are molded to express, inescapably, time after time.

But it is for our own sake as individual women, as well as for the sake of feminism as a political movement, that we need a feminist reevaluation of sexuality. For if we don't want every pleasure and sensation burdened with "meaning," we *do* need to give meaning to our lives, to our collective aspirations, and to the inchoate social change we call the sexual revolution. In the absence of feminist interpretation, we have no way of apprehending any part of this revolution as our own. It becomes someone else's—a victory for men, or for members of sexual "minority groups," or for anyone but the female majority. Or it becomes trivialized as a product of the consumer culture, the counterculture, the pharmaceutical industry—anything rather than being the product of our own desires and efforts.

The consumer culture offers the ultimately meaningless version of sexual revolution. We have seen the importance of the marketplace in institutionalizing the sexual revolution and offering a relatively neutral space within which women can experiment and learn. But the very neutrality of the market on the matter of small choices—do you prefer flavored cream or bondage gear, pornography or more refined erotica?—amounts to a resounding agnosticism on the meaning of our *collective* choices as women. The sexual marketplace offers sexual revolution without revolutionary ideology, innovation without daring, new frontiers without the old risks of exploration. The problem is not that the market makes choices easy, but that it obscures the fact that a more fundamental, social choice is being made at all.

When we participate in a revolution that we do not acknowledge, when we snatch small pleasures out of a context of unchallenged repression, we risk becoming mean-spirited and sly. The result is already apparent in today's mixture of sexual confusion, evasion, and bad faith: Fundamentalists appropriate a more feminist version of sexuality to shore up the patriarchal marriage . . . Male beneficiaries of the sexual revolution declare it over and done with just as they begin to fear that women may be taking their own sexual revolution too far . . . Young women and teenagers claim to disapprove of premarital sex in rising numbers but engage in it anyway, and their denial contributes to the highest rate of teen pregnancy among the industrialized nations . . . Men who have benefited from the sexual double standard join the chorus of voices labeling women who support abortion as selfish or murderous.

This massive bad faith carries real dangers. Hypocrisy can pave the way to new forms of selective repression—of the promiscuous, the "deviant," or those who are merely honest. Denial can open new possibilities for sexual exploitation, as what cannot be spoken cannot easily be protested. And evasion guarantees that sex will slip back into the old morass of mystery, obfuscation, and false and oppressive meanings.

What, finally, are we afraid of when we stand back from our own sexual revolution, when we leave it unannounced, unclaimed, uncelebrated? Ridicule, perhaps, or a loss of dignity, and for women, dignity is still a scarce and precious resource. If we are feminists, we are under pressure—by no means entirely external pressure—to confine ourselves to the "real issues," the urgent matters of economic survival and political power. If we are simply individual women striving for independence and respect, we often find ourselves working hard just to *appear* hardworking and worthy of being taken seriously. We are afraid of seeming silly, afraid of becoming more vulnerable than we already are.

In a society that holds up an increasingly punitive work ethic above any ethic of love or compassion, it is risky indeed to assert *pleasure*—perhaps especially sexual pleasure—as a legitimate social goal. But to remain silent is to concede to a particular political mentality and view of the world. The same mentality that denies a "free lunch" to hungry schoolchildren seeks to restore the reproductive consequences of sexuality. The same mentality that would require mothers on welfare to "work off" their meager benefits would replace family planning and sex education with "chastity centers." Even on the more liberal fringes of politics, talk of "liberation" or of any expanding sense of human possibility can be dismissed as the dated utopianism of a more naive decade.

Yet it is precisely this punitive mood that most challenges us to pick up the lost thread of sexual liberation. If the "real issues" are economic deprivation, the threat of nuclear holocaust, the destruction of the environment, and so forth down the grimly familiar list, then we should perhaps acknowledge that the issue of human pleasure is not, after all, so marginal or secondary. For the "real issues" only reflect our vast, collective separation from the body, from the earth and other life on it, and from the possibility of delight in ourselves and each other. We may have come to the point where we no longer have the luxury—and puritanism can be a perverse kind of luxury—of dividing what is "real" from what is only personal; what is public, from what is most deeply felt. We may finally be obliged, by the very threats we have created for ourselves, to rethink pleasure as a human goal and reclaim it as a human project.

Notes

Chapter 1

1. Frederick Lewis, "Britons Succumb to 'Beatlemania,' " New York *Times Magazine*, December 1, 1963, p. 124.

2. Timothy Green, "They Crown Their Country with a Bowl-Shaped Hairdo," *Life*, January 31, 1964, p. 30.

3. "How to Kick the Beatle Habit," *Life*, August 28, 1964, p.66.

4. David Dempsey, "Why the Girls Scream, Weep, Flip," New York *Times Magazine*, February 23, 1964, p. 15.

5. Quoted in Nicholas Schaffner, *The Beatles Forever* (New York: McGraw-Hill, 1977), p. 16.

6. "George, Paul, Ringo and John," *Newsweek*, February 24, 1964, p. 54.

7. "What the Beatles Prove About Teen-agers," *U.S. News & World Report*, February 24, 1964, p. 88.

8. "Beatles Reaction Puzzles Even Psychologists," *Science News Letter*, February 29, 1964, p. 141.

9. Betty Friedan, *The Feminine Mystique* (New York: W. W. Norton, 1963), p. 282.

10. Quoted in Schaffner, op. cit., p. 15.

11. "Queen Bee of the High School," *Life*, October 11, 1963, p. 68.

12. Lester D. Crow, Ph.D., and Alice Crow, Ph.D., *Adolescent Development and Adjustment* (New York: McGraw-Hill, 1965), pp. 248–49.

13. Dr. Arthur Cain, *Young People and Sex* (New York: The John Day Co., 1967), p. 71.

14. Pat Boone, *'Twixt Twelve and Twenty: Pat Talks to Teenagers* (Englewood Cliffs, N.J.: Prentice-Hall, 1967 edition), p. 60.

15. Connie Francis, *For Every Young Heart* (Englewood Cliffs, N.J.: Prentice-Hall, 1962), p. 138.

16. Grace and Fred M. Hechinger, *Teen-Age Tyranny* (New York: William Morrow and Co., 1963), p. 54.

17. "Shaping the '60s . . . Foreshadowing the '70s," *Ladies' Home Journal*, January 1962, p. 30.

18. Quoted in Philip Norman, *Shout! The Beatles in their Generation* (New York: Simon and Schuster, 1981), p. 200.

19. Samuel Grafton, "The Twisted Age," *Look*, December 15, 1964, p. 36.

20. Hechingers, op. cit., p. 151.

21. Albert Goldman, *Elvis* (New York: McGraw-Hill, 1981), p. 190.

22. Schaffner, op. cit., p. 9.

23. Goldman, op. cit., p. 191.

24. Quoted in Schaffner, op. cit., p. 17.

25. Quoted in Schaffner, op. cit., p. 16.

26. Ellen Willis, *Beginning to See the Light* (New York: Alfred A. Knopf, 1981), p. 63.

Chapter 2

1. Jacqueline Susann, *The Valley of the Dolls* (New York: Bantam, 1966), pp. 2–3.

2. Betty Friedan, *The Feminine Mystique* (New York: W. W. Norton, 1963), p. 261.

3. Ibid., p. 263.

4. Alfred C. Kinsey, Wardell B. Pomeroy, and Clyde E. Martin, *Sexual Behavior in the Human Female* (Philadelphia: W. B. Saunders, 1953), p. 641.

5. Ferdinand Lundberg and Marynia F. Farnham, *Modern Woman: The Lost Sex* (New York: Harper and Bros., 1947), p. 269.

6. Susann, op. cit., p. 174.

7. Th. H. Van de Velde, M.D., *Ideal Marriage: Its Physiology and Technique* (New York: Random House, 1961; first printing, 1930), p. 189.

8. Ibid., p. 7.

9. Ibid., p. 242.

10. Drs. Hannah and Abraham Stone, *A Marriage Manual* (New York: Simon and Schuster, 1968; first printing, 1935), p. 233.

11. Dr. David Reuben, *Any Woman Can!* (New York: McKay, 1971), pp. 19, 31.

12. Van de Velde, op. cit., pp. 201–2.

13. Ibid., p. 235.

14. Lundberg and Farnham, op. cit., p. 275.

15. Hendrik M. Ruitenbeek, ed., *Psychoanalysis and Female Sexuality* (New Haven: College and University Press, 1966), p. 11.

16. Ibid., p. 12.

17. Ibid., p. 14.

18. John D'Emilio, *Sexual Politics, Sexual Communities: The Making of a Homosexual Minority in the United States, 1940–1970* (Chicago: University of Chicago Press, 1983).

19. Kermit Mehlinger, M.D., "The Sexual Revolution," *Ebony*, August 1966, pp. 57–62.

20. Helen Gurley Brown, *Sex and the Single Girl* (New York: Pocket Books, 1962), p. 246.

21. Ibid., p. 4.

22. Ibid., p. 206.

23. Ibid., p. 207.

24. Stanlee Miller Coy, *The Single Girl's Book: Making It in the Big City* (Englewood Cliffs, N.J.: Prentice-Hall, 1969), p. 260.

25. Brown, op. cit., p. 215.

26. See Barbara Seaman, *Free and Female: The Sex Life of the Contemporary Woman* (New York: Coward, McCann & Geoghegan, 1972), p. 63, and Judd Marmor, "Some Considerations Concerning Orgasm in the Female," in Ruitenbeek, op. cit., pp. 198–208.

27. Quoted in Patrick McGrady, "Can the Love Doctors Help Your Sex Life?" *Vogue*, November 1972, p. 144.

28. Dr. Leslie Farber, "I'm Sorry, Dear," *Commentary*, November 1964, p. 47.

29. Lundberg and Farnham, op. cit., p. 29.

30. Alix Shulman, "Organs and Orgasms," in Vivian Gornick and Barbara Moran, eds., *Woman in Sexist Society* (New York: Basic Books, 1971), p. 292.

31. Anne Koedt, "The Myth of the Vaginal Orgasm," in Leslie B. Tanner (ed.) *Voices of Women's Liberation* (New York: New American Library, 1971), p. 39.

32. Quoted in Seaman, op. cit., p. 36.

33. Betty Dodson, "Getting to Know Me," *Ms.*, August 1974, p. 106.

34. Norman Mailer, *Prisoner of Sex* (New York: Little Brown, 1971), p. 77.

Chapter 3

1. Richard Meryman, "Troubled Marriage," *Life*, October 2, 1972, p. 56.

2. Steve Carter, *What Every Man Should Know About the New Woman: A Survival Guide* (New York: McGraw-Hill, 1984), p. 40.

3. Th. H. Van de Velde, M.D., *Ideal Marriage: Its Physiology and Technique* (New York: Random House, 1961), p. 145.

4. J, *The Sensuous Woman* (New York: Dell, 1969), p. 22.

5. Robert J. Levin and Amy Levin, "Sexual Pleasure: The Surprising Preferences of 100,000 Women," *Redbook*, September 1975.

6. Chris Weygandt, "The *Oui* Sex Survey: Fellatio," *Oui*, June 1980, p. 83.

7. Ibid., p. 127.

8. Theodore Fischer, "The *Oui* Sex Survey: Cunnilingus," *Oui*, November 1980, p. 48.

9. Shere Hite, *The Hite Report* (New York: Macmillan, 1976), p. 233.

10. Seymour Fisher, *Understanding The Female Orgasm* (New York: Bantam Books, 1973).

11. Helen Kaplan, *The New Sex Therapy* (New York: Brunner/ Mazel, 1974).

12. Gay Talese, *Thy Neighbor's Wife* (New York: Doubleday, 1980), p. 349.

13. Alex Comfort, *The Joy of Sex* (New York: Simon & Schuster, 1972), p. 225.

14. Nancy Friday, *My Secret Garden* (New York: Pocket Books, 1974), p. xi.

15. Lonnie Garfield Barbach, *For Yourself* (New York: Anchor Press/Doubleday, 1976), p. 9.

16. Eva Margolies, *Sensual Pleasure* (New York: Avon Books, 1981), p. 137.

Chapter 4

1. *The Pleasure Chest Compendium of Amourous & Prurient Paraphernalia* (New York: Pleasure Chest, Ltd., 4th edition, 1979), p. 6.

2. Tony Kornheiser, "Oh, Those Calendar Men," Washington *Post,* December 7, 1983, p. B4.

3. Nancy Collins, "Sex and The Single Star," *Rolling Stone,* August 18, 1983, p. 19.

4. Carrie Rickey, "Unholy Trinity," *The Village Voice,* May 25, 1982, p. 52.

5. Jean Callahan, "Video Erotica Comes Home," *Playgirl,* November 1984, p. 78.

6. Michael Korda, "Love Bites and Slaps: What to Make of Them, When to Play the Fantasy Game, When to Draw the Line," *Self,* July 1981, p. 80.

7. Daniel Goleman, "Sexual Fantasies: What Are Their Hidden Meanings?" New York *Times,* February 24, 1984, p. 1.

8. Ibid., p. 1.

9. Ibid., p. 1.

10. Charles Allen Moser, unpublished doctoral dissertation for the Institute for Advanced Study of Human Sexuality, completed August 1979.

11. Pat Califia, "A Secret Side of Lesbian Sexuality," *The Advocate,* December 27, 1979, p. 21.

12. John Leo, "Stomping and Whomping Galore," *Time,* May 4, 1981, p. 73.

Chapter 5

1. Joanne Young Nawn, private conversation, 1982. We would like to thank Ms. Nawn for her telephone discussions on this topic in 1982. All references to her work are part of those discussions.

2. Michael Braun and George Alan Rekers, *The Christian in an Age of Sexual Eclipse* (Wheaton, Ill.: Tyndale House, 1981), pp. 78–79.

3. Quoted in "A Debate on Religious Freedom," Norman Lear and Ronald Reagan. *Harper's,* October 1984, p. 16.

4. Barry Siegel, "Religious Right Grows and Fights," Los Angeles *Times,* May 15, 1985, p. 1; William Greider, "Attack of the Christian Soldiers," *Rolling Stone,* May 9, 1985.

5. "Jerry Falwell's Crusade," by Richard N. Ostling, *Time*, September 2, 1985, p. 50.

6. Braun and Rekers, op. cit., p. 81.

7. Claire Safran, "Can the Total Woman 'Magic' Work for You?" *Redbook*, February 1976, p. 128.

8. Martin E. Marty, "Fundies and Their Fetishes," *Christian Century*, December 8, 1976, p. 11.

9. Erling Jorstad, *Evangelicals in the White House: The Cultural Maturation of Born Again Christianity 1960–1981* (New York: Edwin Mellen Press, 1981), p. 100.

10. Ibid., p. 102–5.

11. Joyce Maynard, "The Liberation of Total Woman," New York *Times Magazine*, September 28, 1975, p. 106.

12. Marabel Morgan, *Total Joy* (Old Tappan, N.J.: Fleming H. Revell, 1976), p. 143.

13. Maynard, op. cit., p. 58.

14. Emma Goldman, *Living My Life*, Volume II (New York: Dover, 1970), p. 555.

15. H. Page Williams, *Do Yourself a Favor: Love Your Wife* (Plainfield, N.J.: Logos, 1973), pp. 101–2.

16. Ostling, op. cit., p. 51.

17. Tim and Beverly LaHaye, *The Act of Marriage: The Beauty of Sexual Love* (Grand Rapids: Zondervan, 1976), see chap. 5, "The Art of Lovemaking."

18. Ibid., pp. 275–78.

19. Kenneth L. Woodward, "The Bible in the Bedroom," *Newsweek*, Feb. 1, 1982, p. 71.

20. Tim and Beverly LaHaye, op. cit., pp. 33–34.

21. Gini Andrews, *Your Half of the Apple: God and the Single Girl* (Grand Rapids: Zondervan, 1972), pp. 83–84.

22. Edward B. Fiske, "College Aims to Be Fundamentalism's Notre Dame," New York *Times*, Sept. 30, 1981, p. 26.

23. Tim and Beverly LaHaye, op. cit., p. 246.

24. Bob Lardine, "Wonder Woman Finds God, Love and a New Career," New York *Daily News*, February 28, 1982, p. 5.

25. W. Peter Blitchington, *Sex Roles and the Christian Family* (Wheaton, Ill.: Tyndale House, 1980), see chap. 3, "God Had a Purpose in Creating Two Sexes."

26. Barbara Grizzuti Harrison, "The Books that Teach Wives to Be Submissive," *McCall's*, June 1975.

27. Beverly LaHaye, *The Spirit-Controlled Woman* (Eugene, Oregon: Harvest House, 1976), p. 73.

28. Pauline Reage, *The Story of O* (New York: Grove Press, 1965), pp. 15–17.

29. Braun and Rekers, op. cit., p. 114.

30. Williams, op. cit., pp. 17–18.

31. Telephone interview with Dr. Anson Shupe, 1982.

32. Andrews, op. cit., p. 90.

33. Ed Wheat, *Intended for Pleasure* (Grand Rapids: Zondervan, 1981), p. 226.

34. Aimee Sands, producer for WGBH radio, Boston, a three-part series *Women on the Right*, 1982.

35. See Braun and Rekers, op. cit., p. 116; Wheat, *Intended for Pleasure*, p. 162; Andrews, op. cit., p. 30.

36. Andrews, op. cit., p. 84.

Chapter 6

1. Patricia Morrisroe, "Forever Single," *New York*, August 20, 1984.

2. Shere Hite, *The Hite Report on Male Sexuality* (New York: Alfred A. Knopf, 1981), p. 405.

3. "Redbook's Sex Questionnaire: What Readers Had to Say," and "The Redbook Report on Premarital and Extramarital Sex: The End of the Double Standard?" *Redbook*, June and October 1975.

4. Linda Wolfe, *The Cosmo Report: Woman and Sex in the '80s* (New York: Bantam, 1982), p. 153.

5. "Sex and the Married Woman," *Time*, January 31, 1983.

6. "Sex and Success: A Savvy Survey," *Savvy*, October 1985.

7. Roper organization poll for Philip Morris Co., conducted March 1985.

8. George Leonard, "The End of Sex," *Esquire*, December 1982.

9. John Leo, "Sex in the '80s: The Revolution Is Over," *Time*, April 9, 1984.

10. Carol Cassell, *Swept Away: Why Women Fear Their Own Sexuality* (New York: Simon & Schuster, 1984), pp. 99–100.

11. Wendy Holloway, "Heterosexual Sex: Power and Desire for the Other," in Sue Cartledge and Joanna Ryan, eds., *Sex and Love:*

New Thoughts on Old Contradictions (London: The Women's Press, 1983).

12. Wolfe, op. cit., pp. 247–48.

13. Morrisroe, op. cit.

14. "Second Thoughts on Being Single," *NBC Reports,* April 25, 1984.

15. Barbara Creatura, "Sketches from the Single Life," *Cosmopolitan,* March 1984, p. 221.

16. Erica Jong, *Parachutes and Kisses* (New York: New American Library, 1984), p. 2.

17. Elizabeth Pearson-Griffiths, "The Pill + 25," Interview with Jong in *US,* June 3, 1985.

18. Justine DeLacy, "Germaine Greer's New Book Stirs a Debate," New York *Times,* March 5, 1984.

19. Germaine Greer, *The Female Eunuch* (New York, McGraw-Hill, 1970), pp. 322–25.

20. Germaine Greer, *Sex and Destiny: The Politics of Human Fertility* (New York: Harper & Row, 1984), pp. 111–13.

21. Linda Gordon, "Bringing Back Baby," *The Nation,* May 26, 1984.

22. Ellen Kessner, "The Delights of Sexual Mystery," *Cosmopolitan,* September 1984.

23. "Second Thoughts on Being Single," op. cit.

24. Alice Kahn Ladas, Beverly Whipple, and John D. Perry, *The G Spot and Other Recent Discoveries About Human Sexuality* (New York: Holt, Rinehart and Winston, 1982).

25. Nick Freudenberg, "AIDS and Health Education," *HealthPAC Bulletin,* Vol. 16, No. 4, July–August 1985, p. 29.

26. Jon Nordheimer, "With AIDS About, Heterosexuals Are Rethinking Casual Sex," New York *Times,* March 22, 1986, p. 7.

27. Lynne Segal, "Sensual Uncertainty, or Why the Clitoris Is Not Enough," in Cartledge and Ryan, eds., *Sex and Love.*

28. Amber Hollibaugh, "Desire for the Future: Radical Hope in Passion and Pleasure," in Carole S. Vance, ed., *Pleasure and Danger: Exploring Female Sexuality* (Boston: Routledge & Kegan Paul, 1984), p. 403.

29. Shulamith Firestone, *The Dialectic of Sex: The Case for Feminist Revolution* (New York: Bantam, 1971), p. 227.

Bibliography

Altman, Dennis, *The Homosexualization of America* (New York: Beacon, 1983).

Andrews, Gini, *Your Half of the Apple: God and the Single Girl* (Grand Rapids: Zondervan, 1972).

Barbach, Lonnie and Levine, Linda, *Shared Intimacies: Women's Sexual Experiences* (New York: Bantam, 1980).

Belz, Carl, *The Story of Rock* (New York: Harper Colophon, 1972).

Blitchington, W. Peter, *Sex Roles and the Christian Family* (Wheaton, Ill.: Tyndale House, 1980).

Blumstein, Philip, and Schwartz, Pepper, *American Couples* (New York: William & Morrow, 1983).

Braun, Michael, and Rekers, George Alan, *The Christian in an Age of Sexual Eclipse: A Defense Without Apology* (Wheaton, Ill.: Tyndale House, 1981).

Cartledge, Sue and Ryan, Joanna, eds., *Sex and Love: New Thoughts on Old Contradictions* (London: The Woman's Press, 1983).

Cassell, Carol, *Swept Away: Why Women Fear Their Own Sexuality* (New York: Simon & Schuster, 1984).

Comfort, Alex, ed., *The Joy of Sex* (New York: Crown Publishers, 1972).

De Beauvoir, Simone, *The Second Sex* (New York: Vintage, 1952).

Dworkin, Andrea, *Pornography: Men Possessing Women* (New York, Perigee, 1981).

Dworkin, Andrea, *Right Wing Women* (New York: Perigee, 1983).

Eisenstein, Zillah R., *Feminism and Sexual Equality: Crisis in Liberal America* (New York: Monthly Review Press, 1984).

Epstein, Barbara Leslie, *The Politics of Domesticity: Women, Evan-

gelism, and Temperance in Nineteenth-Century America (Middletown, Conn.: Wesleyan University Press, 1981).

Firestone, Shulamith, *The Dialectics of Sex* (New York: Bantam, 1971).

Foucault, Michel, *The History of Sexuality, Vol. 1: An Introduction* (New York: Vintage, 1980).

Friday, Nancy, *My Secret Garden: Women's Sexual Fantasies* (New York: Pocket Books, 1974).

Friday, Nancy, *Men in Love, Men's Sexual Fantasies: The Triumph of Love Over Rage* (New York: Delacorte, 1980).

Friedman, Scarlet, and Sarah, Elizabeth, eds., *On The Problem of Men: Two Feminist Conferences* (London: The Women's Press, 1982).

Gay, Peter, *The Bourgeois Experience: Victoria to Freud, Vol. 1, Education of the Senses* (New York: Oxford University Press, 1984).

Greer, Germaine, *The Female Eunuch* (New York: McGraw-Hill, 1980).

Greer, Germaine, *Sex and Destiny* (New York: Harper & Row, 1984).

Griffin, Susan, *Pornography and Silence* (New York: Harper & Row, 1981).

Hadden, Jeffrey K. and Swann, Charles E., *Prime Time Preachers: The Rising Power of Televangelism* (Reading, Pa.: Addison Wesley, 1981).

Hite, Shere, *The Hite Report on Male Sexuality,* (New York: Alfred A. Knopf, 1981).

Hite, Shere, *The Hite Report* (New York: Macmillan, 1976).

Hunt, Morton, *Sexual Behavior in the Seventies* (Chicago: Playboy Press, 1974).

J, *The Sensuous Woman* (New York: Dell, 1969).

Jong, Erica, *Fear of Flying* (New York: Holt, Rinehart & Winston, 1973).

Jong, Erica, *Parachutes and Kisses* (New York: New American Library, 1984).

Jorstad, Erling, *Evangelicals in the White House: The Cultural Maturation of Born Again Christianity, 1960–1981* (New York: Edwin Mellen Press, 1981).

LaHaye, Tim and Beverly, *The Act of Marriage: The Beauty of Sexual Love* (Grand Rapids, Zondervan, 1976).

LaHaye, Beverly, *The Spirit-Controlled Woman* (Eugene, Oregon: Harvest House, 1976).

LaHaye, Tim, *Understanding the Male Temperament* (Charlotte, N.C.: Commission Press, 1977).

Lederer, Laura, ed., *Take Back The Night: Women on Pornography* (New York: Bantam, 1982).

Marsden, George, *Fundamentalism and American Culture: The Shaping of Twentieth-Century Evangelicalism, 1870–1925,* (New York: Oxford University Press, 1980).

Masters, William H. and Johnson, Virginia E., *Human Sexual Response* (Boston: Little Brown, 1966).

Mollenkott, Virginia R., *Women, Men and the Bible* (Nashville: Abingdon Press, 1977).

Morgan, Marabel, *The Total Woman* (Old Tappan, N.J.: Fleming H. Revell, 1973).

Morgan, Marabel, *Total Joy* (Old Tappan, N.J.: Fleming H. Revell, 1976).

O'Neill, William L., *Coming Apart: An Informal History of America in the 1960's* (Chicago: Quadrangle, 1971).

Paige, Connie, *The Right to Lifers* (New York: Summit, 1983).

Penner, Clifford and Joyce, *The Gift of Sex: A Christian Guide to Sexual Fulfillment* (Waco, Texas: Word Books, 1981).

Reich, Wilhelm, *The Sexual Revolution: Toward a Self-Governing Character Structure,* trans. from the German by Theodore P. Wolfe (New York: Farrar Straus & Giroux, 1962).

Phillips, Eileen, ed., *The Left and the Erotic* (London: Lawrence & Wishart, 1983).

Seaman, Barbara, *Free and Female: The Sex Life of the Contemporary Woman* (New York: Coward, McCann & Geoghegan, 1972).

Shedd, Charlie and Martha, *Celebration in the Bedroom* (Waco, Texas: Word Books, 1979).

Shupe, Anson, and Stacey, William, *Born Again Politics and the Moral Majority: What Shall We Make of Them?* (New York: Edwin Mellen Press, 1982).

Snitow, Ann; Stansell, Christine, and Thompson, Sharon, eds., *The Powers of Desire* (New York: Monthly Review Press, 1983).

Spence, Helen, *The Beatles* (New York: Crescent Books).

Stimpson, Catherine R. and Person, Ethel Spector, *Women: Sex and Sexuality* (Chicago: Chicago University Press, 1984).

Talese, Gay, *Thy Neighbor's Wife* (New York: Dell, 1980).

Vance, Carol S., ed., *Pleasure and Danger: Exploring Female Sexuality* (Boston: Routledge & Keegan Paul, 1984).

Weeks, Jeffrey, *Sexuality and Its Discontents* (London: Routledge & Keegan Paul, 1985).

Wheat, Ed, *Intended for Pleasure* (Grand Rapids: Zondervan, 1980).

Williams, H. Page, *Do Yourself a Favor: Love your Wife* (Plainfield, N.J.: Logos, 1973).

Wolfe, Linda, *The Cosmo Report: Women and Sex in the '80s* (New York: Bantam, 1982).

Young, Perry Dean, *God's Bullies: Power, Politics and Religious Tyranny* (New York: Holt, Rinehart & Winston, 1982).

Index